THE UNTOLD SECRETS
TO THRIVE AS A LAWYER

The Untold Secrets to Thrive as a Lawyer
Six Steps to Ignite Your Legal Career
Even if You Didn't Go to Harvard or Yale

Judy Selby

Published by Game Changer Publishing

Paperback ISBN: 978-1-963793-59-8
Hardcover ISBN: 978-1-963793-60-4
Digital: ISBN: 978-1-963793-61-1

GC GAME CHANGER
PUBLISHING

www.GameChangerPublishing.com

DEDICATION

*To my parents, Peggy and Bob Selby, and my grandparents,
Mary and Peter Conway, who embodied the blue-collar ethos
of hard work, diligence, competence, and responsibility
throughout their lives.*

Read This First

Just to say thank you for buying and reading my book, I would like to give you a few free bonus gifts, no strings attached!

For Free Gifts, Scan the QR Code:

The Untold Secrets
to Thrive as a Lawyer

Six Steps to Ignite Your Legal Career

Even if You Didn't Go to Harvard or Yale

Judy Selby

GAME CHANGER
PUBLISHING

www.GameChangerPublishing.com

ACKNOWLEDGMENTS

A special thanks to my coach, Ben Newman, who not only introduced me to the concept of "the burn" but also serves as an outstanding model for consistent high performance in service to others by connecting to his own burn.

Thanks also to my fellow members of Uncommon Live and The Standard Elite Mastermind. You inspire me every day with your tireless commitment to continuous learning and constant improvement.

And a huge thank you to Doug Houser, the best mentor and role model a young lawyer could ever have. I remain your biggest fan!

Foreword

In the practice of law, one meets many attorneys on a continuum of talents in a variety of areas of expertise. And sometimes, from the moment you encounter a lawyer, you know they are a cut above, with real expertise, but also the grit, determination, discipline, and resilience to help their clients succeed. That is Judy. I have known her for a number of years, but even before we sat on committees together and worked together on panels, I knew of her.

When I have worked on these matters with her, I have always come away sharper and with more knowledge. Recently, Judy called me and we discussed that she was writing this book. She asked me if I would consider writing a foreword. I immediately said yes because, like all of her personal branding I have seen, I knew this would be top-notch.

It does not disappoint. The secrets no longer remain untold. In six chapters, tracking the entire cycle of law firm life, from landing the law firm job to the mindset one needs to decompress and remove stress, Judy answers six key questions.

The lawyer interested in having a long career, the lawyer midway through their career and searching for the path to self-fulfillment, and lawyers in other settings such as in-house or government will all benefit from digesting the wisdom and action items Judy sets forth in the pages of this book.

As those who follow me on LinkedIn can attest, I read and review many books, including legal practice books and guides to sales. Many books are decent, and there are always takeaways. But in this book, every page has real-life examples of how Judy has succeeded and then some with her "blue collar" approach. You, too, can learn from the best.

Getting ready for the interview? Read Chapter 1 and understand the nonverbal cues and how the interview process goes from pre-interview to post.

You have the job—great. Now, turn to the next chapter and follow Judy's framework to survive, thrive, and separate from the associates' herd.

Differentiating will help you become partnership material, and then developing expertise, credentialing, and building your personal brand will all continue to separate you from the pack.

The great thing about these now-disclosed secrets is that they are all things Judy has done to set herself apart in the tough arena of law practice. One thread stands out to me, and I know it is 100% Judy: throughout all the steps of law firm life outlined in this book, the universal truth is that your work product—whether it's your resume for getting the job, your briefs, or your work on a particular matter—is the best selling point for your career success. Early in the book, Judy tells the true story of a large case that involved numerous insurers, and when it went to trial, only a few were left. The verdict came back for Judy's client, and that led to other counsel reaching out to her and offering her a job at his firm.

The other ingredient that comes through is grit. Judy mentions an article that went viral on a new topic and how it got lots of attention but no business for months. She did not give up; she continued to post and publish.

We are in a stressful profession that has more than one million practicing attorneys in the United States. But reading this book, notating it, and taking steps to put the wisdom to work will help in your career trajectory, and help you with the part of the practice that is sales.

Thank you, Judy, for unveiling what you have learned, for revealing the "secret sauce" so that others may thrive, and for being you. My life and practice are enriched by having you in it, and now lawyers at all points of their careers can benefit and be enriched as well.

- Daniel Cotter
  Member
  Dickinson Wright, PLLC

Table of Contents

Introduction

A Look Inside the Firm

"It's not an interview. You can work here if you want."

I was in my fourth year of practicing law, and we had just come off a ten-week insurance coverage trial. The case started out with seven or eight insurer defendants, but by the time the jury announced that it had reached its verdict and we headed over to the courtroom to learn our fate, only three of us were left. We had a feeling that the trial had gone well, but in the hometown of the corporate plaintiff, a big employer in the area, you never really know.

When the jury foreperson read the verdict, I was frozen. Did I hear that right? But then it sank in. Complete victory for the defendants!

The following week, I got a phone call from the lead attorney for one of the defendants which had settled halfway through the trial. He was a partner at one of the most prestigious law firms in the world and the most prominent lawyer in the country in my practice area.

I'll never forget what he said: "I want you to come work with me. But before you decide, I want you to come in and meet some people in the office. But it's not an interview. You can work here if you want."

A week or so later, I was meeting with one of the partners at that firm, and he asked me a question: "How do you think you'll feel about working here? After all, almost everybody went to Harvard or Yale, and you didn't." For some reason, I didn't even flinch, and frankly, I surprised myself with my answer.

"Doesn't there come a time when it doesn't matter where you went to law school? My sister and I were the first in our family to go to college, and I was the first to go beyond that. I guess I'm a blue-collar lawyer. And I'm very good at what I do."

The concept of a blue-collar lawyer had never even entered my mind before that moment. And I think most people probably don't associate a blue-collar work ethic with the legal profession. But I can tell you, after more than thirty years of practice at both midsize and global law firms, including more than twenty years as a Big Law partner, a blue-collar work ethic can propel you to success at every stage of your legal career.

Over the course of my career, I've been through a lot, and I've seen a lot. I've done things right, and I've done things wrong. I've seen a lot of other lawyers do things right, and I've seen plenty of them do things wrong. I've had amazing role models, both for great ways to do things and for terrible ways to do things. And I've seen lawyers break down in tears or explode in anger because they never developed the endurance and the mindset they needed to handle the pressures of a long-term legal career.

So, I come to you today as a law firm insider, speaking to you from real-world experience.

I have started three practice teams, hired more than a hundred lawyers, interviewed far more than that, and had multimillion-dollar books of business. I pivoted midcareer to an emerging niche practice, where there were no leading attorneys or role models, and rebranded as a premier thought leader in that space. I've won awards, had speaking opportunities around the world, written books and countless articles, handled US trials and international arbitrations, and been featured in prominent publications, including the *Wall Street Journal*, *Fortune*, and multiple legal and insurance trade publications.

I say all this only to impress upon you that none of that would have happened for me if I had not brought to the practice of law the grit, determination, discipline, and mindset my blue-collar family modeled for me every single day.

This book is a testament to the enduring value of a blue-collar ethos in navigating the twists and turns of a legal career. I build upon my three decades of experience and all the lessons I have learned to provide the answers to six key questions that can ignite every stage of your legal career, from your first legal job interview through a law firm partnership. I provide strategies, nitty-gritty tactics, practical tips, and some *A Look Inside the Firm* war stories to help you stand out from the crowd and maintain the drive and discipline you'll need to consistently perform at a high level, no matter how long you've been practicing.

So, what are these six questions? I'm glad you asked! Here they are:

1. *How can I make this firm fall in love with me?*

In Chapter 1, we'll go through the steps you should take before, during, and after law firm job interviews to maximize the opportunities and get an offer, whether you choose to accept it or not.

2. *How can I make the partners' jobs easier?*

Chapter 2 focuses on how to succeed as a law firm associate. This may be the most important chapter of the book. Succeeding as an associate is absolutely foundational to success in the rest of your career, including getting promoted to partnership and honing the skills you'll need to develop your own book of business. This is the stuff they don't teach you in law school, even if you went to Harvard or Yale.

3. *How can I be seen as partnership material?*

To position yourself well for partnership, you'll probably need to do a lot more than consistently provide good legal work. You'll also need to sell yourself, including to people you may have never met, on the idea that you're partnership material. Chapter 3 provides some tried-and-true advice on how to do that.

4. *How do I show appreciation for my clients and make their jobs easier?*

Chapter 4 is all about developing your own book of business and providing excellent service to your clients. The key is to always remember, no matter how senior you are, that you're in the service business. Your job, regardless of your area of legal concentration or your abilities as an attorney, is to develop and maintain excellent client relationships. You do this by making your clients' jobs easier and by consistently showing them that you appreciate them putting their trust in you.

5. *How do I make sure the right people know what I do?*

In Chapter 5, I provide detailed steps on how to brand, and even rebrand, as a go-to expert in your practice area. You'll learn how to build a network and an audience, get quoted in the press, and position yourself as a true thought leader in front of the key people in your practice area or industry.

6. *How can I bring my best self to my work every day, year after year?*

The critical strategies and skills you'll learn in chapters 1 through 5 are not the end of the story. To become your best, to reach your highest potential, you're going to need the right mindset and mental toughness to push through adversity and discomfort and do things you don't "feel like" doing. In chapter 6, I provide the strategies and tactics I've used for years to maintain energy, drive, and determination over decades of high-pressure, high-stakes Big Law practice.

Let's get started!

CHAPTER 1

Land Your Law-Firm Job

How can I make this firm fall in love with me?

A Look Inside the Firm

"Can you see me?"

I logged in to a remote interview with a candidate for an associate position at my firm. After I joined the call, I noticed that the interviewee was already online but that none of my colleagues was online yet. I waved, smiled, and said, "Hi, so nice to meet you."

The candidate responded with a hello but no smile, no wave back, no acknowledgment that another person was actually online. I checked to see if my camera was on because it was a little bit odd. And my camera was, indeed, on. I smiled again, waved again, and still no reaction at all from the candidate. By this point, other interviewers started to join the call as well, and the candidate had the exact same reaction. No change in facial expression at all. We proceeded with the interview, but the candidate's demeanor was a huge distraction. We started trying to come up with some icebreaker-type questions to elicit a more human response, and we got nothing. It was a bit disappointing because the candidate looked really good on paper, so I was looking forward to the interview.

At the end of the interview, we asked typical close-out questions like, "What do you like to do when you're not working?" And the candidate really had a hard time answering those types of questions. Game over. We knew that we couldn't go forward with this particular candidate, despite our pressing need for someone with her qualifications.

When you're interviewing for a law firm position, you will already have been vetted based on your résumé and law school transcript. The working assumption going into the interview is often that you're able to do the job.

The issue then becomes, is this the type of person we want to work with? Is this somebody we will want to see when they walk into the firm kitchen to grab a cup of coffee?

You want to be somebody that people want to see every day when they go to work. It doesn't happen often, but I have seen partners literally excuse themselves just minutes into an interview when they know they just don't like the candidate.

In each of those circumstances, the candidate either demonstrated poor social skills or just plain arrogance.

Whether you're interviewing for your first law firm job or looking to make a lateral move, the goal of any interview is to get an offer. Whether you choose to accept that offer is a completely different question, but your goal should be to get an offer. A recruiter once told me that getting an offer after a job interview is the equivalent of somebody saying "I love you" first. That should be your goal. Whether you accept the offer or not, your goal should be to get the offer.

Your ability to be someone who people want to work with is especially important now that the law firm job market is showing signs of tightening up, and people are graduating from law school with record amounts of debt. This makes it all the more important to put your best foot forward so that you actually have a choice of which firm you would like to join.

Before the Interview

The first thing you can do to increase your chances of getting interviews (and eventually job offers) is to have a well-designed résumé. It should, of course, feature your professional experiences, but it should also highlight things that can make you stand out from your peers, such as involvement in legal or relevant industry associations or your background in competitive sports.

Obviously, you want to keep your résumé free from any typos. It should be short and impactful. And it must be accurate. There is no room for embellishment or exaggeration on your résumé. Highlight any practical or relevant law school classes that you might have taken.

Some people include a list of references in their resumes, while others simply prepare a separate list of references. Regardless, you'll probably need three references, which likely will be professors or former employers. Never list people as references unless you've already cleared it with them. And if a potential employer requests written references, don't be surprised if your references ask you to write the first draft of the letter for them, so start thinking about what those letters should say.

If you have taken courses in law school that are of personal interest to you but not really practical in nature, you may not want to highlight those on your résumé. But if you have taken courses in subject matters that your target law firms specialize in or that are super practical, like e-discovery, by all means, highlight those.

In my practice area, I look for candidates who have taken courses in insurance, privacy, or cyber issues. Because these are hot areas of the law right now, a lot of associate candidates think it's enough to simply say that they're "really interested" in going into those areas. But you'd really get a leg up if you have some demonstrable evidence of that, such as taking on-point law school courses or joining organizations that focus on those issues.

Make sure you have writing samples ready to provide if requested. Don't shoot yourself in the foot by providing writing samples that are poorly written or have typos and errors. Proofread them carefully, and ask someone else to double-check you.

A Look Inside the Firm

"Well, that saved a lot of time."

We had a pressing need for a mid-level associate position with experience in a particular area of the law. We received a résumé from a candidate who looked really great on paper, and it indicated a lot of experience in the area we needed. During the interview, the candidate was extremely personable and answered general questions very well. However I noticed that he was a bit flippant with regard to questions concerning the exact experience we were looking for. This just didn't sit right with us.

To put our minds at rest, we decided to ask for some additional writing samples dealing with the exact specific area of the law in which we were interested. When we got the samples, not only could we immediately tell that the candidate's experience had been embellished both in the résumé and during the interview, but worse, the writing samples were not redacted for case-specific information.

Needless to say, the candidate was immediately disqualified, and, as one of my partners commented afterward, "We saved a lot of time."

Make sure to research the firm and the attorneys you are meeting with in depth before the interview. Go on LinkedIn and observe the type of content they publish, like, or interact with; note who they're connected with; and identify what issues they focus on.

Go to the firm's website and carefully research everything. Run Google searches for the firm and the people you're scheduled to meet so that you're well-prepared when you walk in on game day.

For me in particular, if an associate comes into the interview having researched cyber issues in advance, my interest certainly would be piqued. During a recent interview, it became apparent that the candidate had read many of my recent articles, was well aware of the types of matters I worked on, and even mentioned an award I recently won. This made that candidate stand out among all the other interviews we had that day. Somewhat incredibly, most people don't put in that extra effort.

You also should research the industry that the law firm tends to serve. For example, if the law firm works a lot with the energy sector, identify important legal issues that impact those companies.

Be well prepared to answer the types of questions that are typically asked during interviews. Although you can never predict exactly what questions you'll get, you should be ready to answer basic questions, such as:

- Why did you go to law school?
- What did you like most about law school?
- What did you like least about it?
- What were your favorite classes in law school? Why?
- Why are you interested in our firm?

If you have a work history, even a non-legal-related work history, interviewers may ask you what you liked about your job or what you didn't like about it.

They may also ask you what your biggest strengths and weaknesses are. And they may ask what you like to do outside of work. They may ask you where you see yourself in five years. And if you have any breaks in your résumé, they may ask about what you were doing during that time.

You don't need to have your answers memorized, but you should be ready to discuss the answers in a relaxed, conversational way.

The interviewer may also ask you some questions that are less intuitive. While they probably won't ask a Barbara-Walters-style question about what kind of tree you'd like to be, don't be surprised if they ask you some less intuitive kinds of questions like, "What would your entrance or theme song be?" or "What are you most proud of in your life?"

They may also ask questions about ethical considerations, especially if you have some prior experience at a law firm. These questions are a great opportunity to emphasize your commitment to ethical conduct. If you've had to navigate an ethical dilemma, discuss how you handled it and how you upheld professional integrity throughout that process.

Before you even start your job search, it's important to take a hard look at all your social media and other online content. I can guarantee you that firms are looking at all of that. They're conducting Google searches. They're looking at Facebook, Instagram, TikTok, and other platforms where you may have posted online content. Clean all that up before you start your job search. You don't want anything controversial there, and you definitely don't want every picture of you to be at a party with a solo cup in your hand. Take some time to make sure that all the public-facing content on your social media accounts portrays you the way you want to be portrayed and the way you think a law firm would want to see you.

At this point, I would be remiss not to mention that taking public positions on hot-button political issues may be risky. There have been some very recent examples of law school students taking public positions on certain issues, and their job offers were publicly rescinded and made national news. This obviously is a personal choice. It's your decision, but like anything else in life, you really should consider all the ramifications of your actions and recognize that there are risks if you decide to post content on divisive or potentially controversial issues such as politics.

Well in advance of any interview, start thinking about what questions you can ask the interviewer. Tailor those questions to convey your professional responsibility, work ethic, and drive.

Avoid questions about how many vacation or sick days you get, or what happens if you don't meet the billable-hour requirement. Asking how the firm builds camaraderie and enhances its culture with social events would be great, but focusing on how many happy hours the firm hosts may not be your best move.

Even though you've prepared a list of questions in advance, don't pull out your list during the interview. Your questions should flow naturally from the discussion and appear organic, even if you had them prepared in advance.

But I believe it's important to ask at least one question at the end of an interview. Otherwise, you may appear disinterested or unprepared.

Make sure you dress appropriately for the interview. These days, especially because so many people work remotely, lawyers sometimes wear hoodies, T-shirts, and jeans to work. This, however, cannot be you.

You must always dress professionally for an interview, whether it's remote or in person. It's highly likely that you will be the only person dressed up during the interview, especially a remote interview. But that's okay. It's expected that the candidate will dress professionally.

Although you want to dress well, you don't want to appear to be showy or ostentatious. I was once taking part in an interview with several of my colleagues in a large conference room. The candidate was escorted in and was dressed very well. As she settled into her seat, she placed an expensive designer bag on the table. Honestly, I didn't even notice, and I'm sure she meant nothing by it. But one of my colleagues was instantly turned off.

She thought the candidate was being showy, questioned whether she even needed to work, and instantly disqualified that candidate. She was overruled, however, but it was an unnecessary issue that we had to deal with, which is why I caution that you should be aware of any unintended signals that you may put out when it comes to your dress or accessories.

During the Interview

Arrive a little bit early for your interview and do your best to convey ease and confidence when you walk in. If you're asked to wait in the lobby before being called in for an interview, don't waste the opportunity by scrolling through your phone. Instead, use this as your chance to observe! Be on the lookout for clues about how it would feel to work there.

How are people dressed? How do they interact with each other? Do they smile and say hi to you or otherwise acknowledge you as they pass by?

These could be important signs of the firm's culture. Consider if this is the type of environment where you can see yourself working and thriving.

Even if you're picking up negative vibes or a feeling that this may not be the firm for you, your goal for the interview should remain the same. You want to get an offer. Whether you accept it or not is a different question.

Look at each interview as a valuable exercise where you can gain knowledge, experience, and improve your interviewing skills, even if you realize that you have no intention of accepting an offer.

Smile and be friendly to everyone you interact with during the interview process, including the people you meet when you first walk in the door. If you're rude or unfriendly to the receptionist, you can be sure that the decision-makers will hear about it. Some attorneys, myself included, make a point to go out to the lobby and ask the receptionist, and other people who interacted with the candidate, what they thought of you. We ask: "How did the candidate interact with you?" "Were they nice to you?" "Were they respectful to you?"

Even if you've ruled out a firm after your interview, keep in mind that lawyers move around. They chat with lawyers at other firms. You want everyone you meet, whether in an interview setting or otherwise, to have nothing but good things to say about you.

During the actual interview, it may become apparent that at least some of the interviewers may not have read your résumé in advance. You'll see attorneys sitting there scanning your résumé for the first time during the interview. I have seen many, many situations where attorneys were handed a résumé and asked to run into a conference room for an interview two minutes in advance. Other times, the attorneys simply may not have taken the time to read your résumé in advance.

In those situations, it's key to look for opportunities to highlight the most important parts of your résumé because they may not otherwise be recognized by the interviewers.

Be ready to discuss every detail of your résumé. Anything that's included in your résumé is fair game for questions. You must be able to easily and confidently speak about everything on your résumé. If you can't, you risk looking unprepared or, at worst, inauthentic.

If the interviewer asks a question that you don't know the answer to, be honest and say so. Attempting to bluff or provide an incorrect answer can really backfire on you.

Throughout the interview process, be on the lookout for nonverbal cues, both good and bad. But also be aware of the nonverbal cues that you are putting out. Make sure you smile, nod in agreement or acknowledgment when somebody else is talking, lean in on your seat when it's appropriate, and show that you are fully engaged in the process. Be aware of your posture and hand gestures during an interview. Don't twirl your hair, fidget with a pen, or do anything that would become a distraction. Make sure your phone is on silent, and do *not* hold your phone in your hand. Make eye contact throughout the interview with all the interviewers.

Try to keep the discussion focused on your professional qualifications as much as possible. If a personal issue comes up, exercise discretion about what you share. But at the same time, as I've noted, you want to be human when you walk in there because people are looking for people they want to work with as human beings.

For example, you might walk into somebody's office for an interview, and as you take your seat, you look around and see some pictures or "knick-knacks" around the office that present some clues as to the interviewer's personality and interests. If you see a picture of a baseball player or an autographed football, you may say, "Oh, I see you're a Yankee fan," or "You're a Chiefs fan." Those things can be really nice icebreakers. Be careful not to go down a rabbit hole of personal chitchat, but a few touches of personal interactions can humanize the experience and create some bonding between you and the interviewer.

Never be negative during your interview. The interviewer may ask you why you're interested in leaving your current position, or how you liked working at a prior position or internship. Do your best to avoid criticizing your employer, your colleagues, or saying anything bad about anybody at your firm. If you are leaving your firm due to some kind of conflict or other negative reasons, think ahead about appropriate things that you can say as to why you're interested in leaving that won't be perceived as a red flag during an interview. You might say that you're looking to focus on another area of the law and that this firm provides better opportunities for that. Or there might be something in particular about this law firm that's of interest to you.

For example, maybe the new firm has a better national footprint or a global platform that would be helpful to your practice. The firm may generally be seen as a leader in a specific area of the law. It's really important to remember that there are a lot of lawyers, but the legal community in any given city or specialty area can actually be pretty small. A lot of lawyers know each other, talk to each other, and meet and network with each other even though they're not at the same law firm. It will serve you well throughout your career to remember that once words leave your mouth, you remain responsible for them, but you lose control over them. And you never know what may be repeated to others.

A Look Inside the Firm

"If you hire me, what would I have to do so you'll say, 'That was the best hire we ever made?'"

I have hired dozens of attorneys throughout my career and interviewed far more than that. This was by far the best question a candidate ever asked me during an interview. When you think about it, it shows you that this candidate was positive, forward-thinking, and looking to get a head start on ways that he could excel, even before he got the job. He recognized that getting hired was simply the first step, and he was looking for an edge to ensure that his performance would be phenomenal. He was hired, and as you might expect, he did not disappoint.

If you can relate your questions to the particular interviewers, that would probably be well received. After all, everybody loves talking about themselves.

You might ask in the interview:

"What do you like most about this firm?"

"What drew you to this law firm?"

"What is a typical day for an associate like?"

"What is your typical day like?"

"What makes a new associate really stand out in your eyes?"

Be careful about any personal stories that you may choose to share. Even if you're feeling really comfortable in any given interview, remember it's a job interview, so it's not the right time to tell stories about high school pranks, misdemeanors, and other shenanigans in your life, such as flooding a gym before a big basketball game. (No, I did not make that up.)

Emphasize your experience and things you're especially good at. Make sure you do that in your résumé, but if the interviewer didn't read your résumé, try to focus the discussion on important things in your background. Like your excellent experience with legal writing and research, or the client-facing experiences you have had.

Highlight the role you actually played in those interactions, like presenting on a certain issue or making recommendations to a client. If you happen to have any courtroom or deposition experience, mention that as well.

You should also look for ways to emphasize your ability to work well on a team. Collaboration is a key skill to success in a law firm and in delivering good client work, so find a way to discuss where you've contributed to the success of any team projects. In my experience, people who come from a background of team sports typically become collaborative lawyers, so consider adding any team-sport experiences to your résumé and find a way to highlight that during the interview.

It should go without saying, but it's important to note that you shouldn't say things that could come across as insulting to the firm or its lawyers. Things like, "Will I get stuck working with one person at the law firm?" or "I don't want to do this particular type of work because it's boring and not challenging." (And yes, people really do say things like this in interviews.)

If, during your pre-interview research, you find out that the firm has been embroiled in some kind of controversy or has had bad press, perhaps about a personnel issue or a high-profile matter the firm is handling, I suggest that you do not raise those issues during an interview. Remember, your goal is to get a job offer—whether you want it or not.

But if there are things that trouble you about the firm, consider raising those issues with your recruiter or with the firm's HR department, but not during a particular interview with individual lawyers.

Don't interrupt when an interviewer is speaking. It's often said that when interviewers who talk a lot during an interview walk away saying, "Boy, that was a great interview." So let them speak, but still look for ways to interject when it's appropriate if you have a point worth making.

Don't drop any F-bombs. Coarse language has become much more common and less taboo in lots of different settings, including law firms, but I would strongly guard against using it in an interview, even if one of your interviewers uses a few choice words during the interview. You will not be judged by the same standard.

Make sure you have a good handshake. This goes for women as well. A firm handshake sends a vibe of self-confidence and friendliness. A weak or limp shake can really be a killer. People absolutely hate a limp handshake, and they may even talk about it after the interview.

Make sure that you appear organized and prepared during the interview. You should easily be able to pull out a copy of your résumé, transcript, or writing sample if the interviewer asks for them. Fumbling around for your documents during an interview can make you look disorganized and unprepared. And be sure you bring extra copies of important documents with you in case there are multiple interviewers who need copies.

A Special Note to More Recent Gen Lawyers

Here's a revised version with corrected grammar:

According to some, lawyers from more recent generations may particularly struggle with in-person interviews. There are a number of speculated causes for these purported hang-ups, including COVID, but generally, some articles claim that younger generation grads aren't really fond of making small talk, may not be relaxed in professional environments, and can feel a little bit uncomfortable when they're not holding their phone.

If this speaks to you, the good news is that with some extra preparation, you can still ace your interviews. Consider these tips:

- **Practice interviews.** Convince your friends, family, or someone from your law school career office to practice with you. If you practice with friends, please take it seriously. Everybody really has to play their part if it's going to be of any value to you.

- **Try to get an internship while you're in school.** You'll get used to how people work in a professional setting, including how they interact with each other in person.

- **Get used to putting your phone away.** Put your phone down for thirty minutes or more at a time on a regular basis so you don't feel out of sorts during an interview when you're not clutching your phone.

- **Practice talking to people you don't know.** Go into networking events or other social settings with a goal of being more *interested* in other people than being *interesting* yourself. This completely takes the pressure off you! Look to *give* and not *get*.

- **Start conversations with strangers.** Be on the lookout for random situations throughout your day to talk to people you don't know. This can start to make you more comfortable in career-related situations. Practice small talk. Maybe say a polite hello to someone in the elevator, or compliment someone on their cute dog when you're walking outside. Or maybe offer a brief comment about the weather to somebody as you're waiting in line at Starbucks. Of course, you have to be safe about this but try to get out of your shell and increase your comfort level when speaking with people you don't know.

It's also key to remember the distinct advantages you may have if you're part of a digital-native generation! You probably have skills that can be quite valuable to any employer, including a law firm.

For example, you may be super experienced and comfortable with technology. If you have proficiency in legal software and research platforms, make a point to emphasize that during the interview and in your résumé.

The key thing to remember, though, is that law firms generally look for people they will enjoy working with, who can grow with the firm, and who can develop client relationships. Your ability to effectively interact with firm employees and lawyers throughout the interview process can go a long way to show that you're up to the job!

After the Interview

Promptly send a thank-you email after your interview. I mean the same day while you're still fresh in the minds of the interviewers. I know some people think that thank-you notes are old-fashioned, but you should think of it as another opportunity for you to stand out.

If you talked to different people in the law firm, tailor your message to each person you met. Don't send the same note to each person. In my experience, lawyers circulate thank-you emails to the other interviewers as well as to the firm's hiring personnel. So, put some thought into it. If possible, mention something the person said, or a funny or important moment during the interview.

If you don't get an offer from the law firm, consider asking for feedback from the firm, or if you're working with a headhunter, ask the headhunter to try to get that feedback for you. For example, if you were the candidate who never smiled throughout the interview, that would be some really good feedback to have.

Action Steps

- Before the interview, think about how you can showcase strong social skills and genuine interest in the firm's work, attorneys, culture, and values.

- Before, during, and after your interviews, focus on the details. Prepare and follow up better than anyone else.

CHAPTER 2

Succeed as an Associate

How can I make the partners' jobs easier?

Congratulations, you got the job! But getting the job is very different from being great at the job and keeping the job. This chapter will give you the upper hand to becoming a rock-star associate.

This is the stuff they don't teach you in law school. You'll need this advice. Even the best law firms, the ones with the greatest reputation for culture and firm values, can be difficult places to work. That's just the nature of the job.

There are client deadlines and court deadlines that you have no control over. The practice of law is packed with pressure, but by implementing the advice in this chapter, you'll position yourself to minimize the pressure, stand out, and become one of your firm's go-to associates.

A Look Inside the Firm

"That's why I like working with you!"

It was early on a Monday morning during my first year as a lawyer. I was walking down the hallway of my law firm, and I crossed paths with the biggest-named partner in the firm. I had worked with him a bit already, so he knew who I was.

He brightly said, "Morning, Judy! How are you?"

I smiled and said, "Morning, Dave. I'm great! How about you?"

Dave stopped dead in his tracks, turned halfway around, and said: "That's why I like working with you! You're always upbeat. You always say you're great. You never say 'I'm fine' or 'I'm okay.'"

I remember this like it was yesterday, and it serves as a great example of spontaneous mentoring! Dave's comments provided super valuable insight as to what partners are looking for in an associate. Believe me, it wasn't contrived when I said "I'm great." It's just my personality.

At that moment, I came to understand that what you say about yourself and the vibe you put out 100 percent impacts how other people view you. And when you think about it, nobody wants to be around a negative, complaining person. They drain the energy out of the people around them.

People, especially successful people, are naturally drawn to positive, upbeat people. They give off an energy that people find attractive and want to be around. When I have to interact with a negative, complaining person, I find myself taking a deep breath and bracing myself in advance. I'm also thinking about ways to keep the conversation short. But I actually do my best not to deal with them in the first place.

I've never seen a person reach any level of success in the law by being a negative and complaining person. One of those people who are always on the lookout for something to be offended by. This type of person is difficult and annoying to work with, and they absolutely do not attract clients.

Even if you're going through a hard time, maybe something with your family or personal life, try to give off an air that you are happy to be at work, that you are enjoying your experience there, especially as a young associate.

Also, another word of caution. Exercise a high level of discretion concerning how much you want to share in the workplace about anything that's going wrong in your personal life.

Be aware of the energy you're giving off, and make sure you won't be seen as an unhappy, high-drama, or high-maintenance person. And even if it's not your personality to say that you're "great," perhaps you should consider doing that, even if it doesn't feel true when you say it. And as a bonus, you might just find that you actually start feeling great if you say it enough!

A Look Inside the Firm

"I took care of that."

I had just started working with a mid-level associate on a complex matter. He and I were on a conference call with clients, during which we agreed to have a follow-up call at a certain date and time the following week.

After the clients left the call, I asked the associate to please send out an invitation for that next meeting. With a smile, he said, "Oh, I already took care of that."

Sure enough, I looked at my email, and the invitation to the meeting he'd sent was sitting right there. He'd sent it out immediately once the date and time were agreed with the client. This was one less issue that I had to think about after the call.

Look for opportunities to reduce the things partners have to worry about—their cognitive load. You may not realize it, but partners typically are responsible for many, many more cases than you are, and they typically work with multiple associates. Be the associate who does the little things that make the partners' lives easier and make them want to keep working with you.

Think of areas where you can do simple things without having to be asked in advance. I was once working with a partner on a large matter that was headed to trial. Lots of other law firms were involved in the case as well, and we had a large joint-defense group, which started to meet more and more frequently as the trial date approached.

As the lead associate on the case, I attended all the meetings myself. But as the trial date grew closer, the partner I was working with also needed to attend the meetings. We eventually went through a ten-week trial and won. Our client was ecstatic!

Right after the trial ended, I had my review. Everything was super positive, except for one thing. The partner I worked with on the trial pointed out that I'd never saved him a seat next to me at the joint-defense group meetings, so we were unable to easily communicate during those readings. Man… It was such an obvious thing that I should have thought about, but I absolutely didn't.

A Look Inside the Firm

"Where did you get that number?"

One day as a first-year lawyer, I was summoned to the office of an important senior partner to discuss a draft appellate brief I had prepared. I was ready for this meeting! I knew the case was cold. I was prepared to explain why I organized the arguments as I did.

I sat down across from him. He pointed to the case number in the caption on the first page of the brief and asked, "Where did you get that number?" I was a bit thrown away by the question. I did not expect it at all. I muttered, "My secretary put that in."

Strike one.

He then asked if I double-checked it.

No, I didn't.

Strike two.

The only good thing about this situation was that, despite being mortified, I somehow had enough sense *not* to say that I had assumed the number was correct. That probably would have been strike three.

It turns out the number was right, but that didn't matter. I hadn't taken complete ownership of my work, and I embarrassed myself in front of his senior partner. I'm embarrassed now just thinking about this, even though it was over thirty years ago! But it was a key lesson that I get to share with you now. Take responsibility and ownership over every detail of your work. And never assume anything!

Another key point is to always remember exactly what job you're being asked to do in any given situation. If you're a very junior lawyer who has been invited to a meeting with more senior lawyers, for example, you're likely there in a support role. Your primary role may be to make sure the presentation is working, everyone has the right documents, and to take good notes. Of course, you'll learn from being in the room and hearing the discussion among the senior lawyers, but never forget what *your* job is in that situation.

A Look Inside the Firm

"He's grazing again."

Our team was preparing for a high-stakes trial, which meant having many long days of meetings with expert witnesses in large conference rooms. Breakfast, lunch, and snacks were typically provided throughout the day. These were high-pressure meetings where we had to carefully consider the evidence each expert could provide concerning complex technical issues. We also had to explore potential weaknesses in our case and where our experts' background, experience, and presentation style might be exploited by our opposing counsel.

The most junior member of our team was a brand-new associate whose main job at the meetings was to take really detailed notes. That was it!

We would need to look at those notes afterward to formulate our strategy, and provide reports and recommendations to our client.

This associate was a very competent lawyer. And a super nice guy. However, during these high-stakes meetings, he seemed much more interested in eating than doing his job!

He spent most of the day walking around the food table, grazing, deciding what he was going to eat next, and then taking overflowing plates of food back to the conference table to eat.

This became a major distraction to everybody in the meetings, which was bad enough, but we also weren't getting the quality of the notes that we needed from him. It wasn't long before we replaced him on the team.

Remember what your role is in every situation and prioritize doing your job. Be self-aware and never *ever* become a distraction.

Even if you've just started practicing, it's not too early to demonstrate that you're the type of person who might develop into a firm partner. It's not just about doing great work. It's also about showing you care about the firm and the people who work there.

A Look Inside the Firm

"Sure, I'm happy to help."

When I was a first year associate, I volunteered for a program offered by the local District Attorney's office. Every week, the DA would assign a relatively simple matter for the volunteer to handle, under the DA's supervision. The program provided real world trial experience that can be hard to come by for new lawyers at a big law firm.

One Friday afternoon, I was assigned two small misdemeanor cases that were scheduled for trial on Monday morning. I prepared for hours and hours all weekend, but when I arrived at the courthouse on Monday morning, I was informed that neither case was going forward. I have to admit I was somewhat relieved as I started to head out of the courthouse. Just as I was about to hit the revolving door, I saw the assigning attorney from the DA's office standing there with a clipboard. She called me over and told me that one of her staff attorneys was delayed and asked if I would handle a case that was going to trial in two hours.

Every part of me wanted to say no, make up some excuse, and head back to the office. But a little voice inside me said, *Just do it! And if it doesn't go well, you'll have a built-in excuse.* I really didn't want to say yes, But I said I would do it.

I reviewed the file in a phone booth and then headed into the courtroom for what turned out to be a two-day trial. To increase the drama—at least from my perspective—a class of fifth graders just happened to be touring the courthouse that day. Since mine was the only trial going on that day, they all came to observe! On the second day, a group of secretaries from my law firm came to watch. Needless to say, I was a wreck!

When the trial was over, I was beyond relieved, but I was also proud that I somehow managed to say yes when I was asked to handle it. That experience ended up being super valuable for me and a real confidence boost very early in my career.

Step up and take opportunities when they are offered to you, and don't be ruled by temporary feelings of anxiety, doubt, or fear. As Eleanor Roosevelt said, do the thing you fear. It's one of the best ways to build your confidence and your skill set. And I think you'll discover that you are stronger and more competent than you realized.

A Look Inside the Firm

"That's what I'm talking about! Partnership mentality!"

One morning, when I was a first-year lawyer, I was in the office kitchen, making a cup of tea and chatting with another associate. As we were chatting, I happened to notice that there was some water on the linoleum floor. As we continued talking, I grabbed some paper towels and cleaned it up so no one would slip. At the time, I didn't realize that a senior partner was sitting at a table on the other side of the room.

When he saw what I had done, he came rushing over to us, pointing to the floor, saying, "That's what I'm talking about! That's what I'm talking about!" The other associate and I looked up, having no idea what he was talking about. And he said something I'll never forget: "Partnership mentality! That's what we like to see. You didn't have to do that."

What a lesson that was for us to learn as young lawyers. I had never heard the term "partnership mentality" before, but I knew exactly what he meant once he said it. And it changed the way I approached my job, even as a first-year associate.

Make Yourself a Go-To Associate

Becoming a go-to associate takes much more than doing excellent legal work. That's table stakes. It's the intangible, little things that certain associates do on a regular basis that make partners' lives easier and make them stand out among their peers.

Here's a list of things to do that can supercharge your reputation as a go-to associate. But I have to say in advance that none of this is rocket science. This is just basic common sense. But you would be shocked to know that very few associates actually do these things. This means that if you do them, you will really stand out and accelerate your reputation as an indispensable associate who partners will want on their team.

- **Never forget that you are in the service business.** And just as a huge part of your job is to make the partners' jobs easier, a huge part of a partner's job is to make their clients' jobs easier. That's just the reality of being in the professional services business.

- **Always be prepared at meetings.** Know what the meeting is about, and be prepared to discuss relevant issues. I attended an important meeting several years ago with some of the most senior leaders of the firm. The meeting had been on all our calendars for weeks. A senior associate was also in attendance. When he walked into the conference room, he sat down and said, "What's this meeting about?" He was let go shortly after that, but not for that one mess-up. But that incident did confirm a pattern of behavior on his part, and that meeting happened to be the proverbial last straw.

- **Bring a legal pad and pen to every meeting.** Bring extras if you're being joined by senior lawyers at the meeting in case they forget.

- **Know the facts of your case better than anyone else.** When I was assigned to new matters as a young lawyer, the first thing I would do is draft a chronology of key events and a list of the key players involved in the case. These chronologies often became known as the Bible of those cases. And no one knew the facts of those cases better than I did since I drafted everything from scratch.

- **Put your phone down during meetings before you're asked to do it.** If you're asked to attend an in-person meeting, this can be your chance to shine. I guarantee that you most definitely will not do that if you're not 100% focused on the meeting! If you're sitting scrolling on your phone during the meeting, at best, you'll send the wrong message. At worst, you'll be asked in front of everyone to put your phone away or to leave the meeting.

- **Show partners they can trust you by doing what you say you will do.** As partners begin to trust you more and more, you'll get better assignments with greater responsibility, including client-facing opportunities, which I believe should be the long-term goal of every associate who wants to be elevated to partnership.

- **Partners should never, *ever* have to wonder if you're really going to do what you've been asked to do.** When work has been assigned to you, the partner should be able to check it off their list instead of needing to add "check in about the assignment" to yet another list. Remember, you want to lighten the partners' cognitive load, not add to it!

- **Never, *ever* get chased for work.** If there are reasons—and they should be really good reasons—why you can't meet the deadline, talk to the partner as far in advance of the due date as possible. Don't tell them the day the assignment is due that you don't think you can deliver it on time. Remember, partners are often juggling lots of different cases from a variety of clients. They likely are working with many different associates, and they have court and client deadlines they need to keep in mind. Partners will often set aside special time to review the project you're due to submit. When your work is late, it can throw off many other projects the partner is working on.

- **Be careful not to go off on a tangent when you're conducting legal research.** Go to the assigning partner if you suspect you might be doing that, and ask for clarification. They may be able to save you time and get you back on track to meet your deadline. Or the partner may assign another attorney to help you to get the work done.

- **Most deadlines imposed by partners are not some random, arbitrary date.** Remember that there are usually good reasons for the deadline that's set, and those reasons may be driven by clients or judges.

- **Look for ways to over-deliver.** For example, if you promise a draft by Friday, turning it in on Thursday may help you to look like a superstar.

- **Be proactive.** Always ask yourself, "What's the next thing I can do to help move the ball forward in this case?" Anticipate what the partner or client may need next. This becomes easier to do as you gain more experience.

- **Always name documents and PDFs with a description.** When you're sending documents or PDFs to a partner or a client, make sure you name them in a helpful way so the recipient will know what they are. Think about it. If somebody sends you an email with five PDFs, and they're all named with some random numerical sequence, you have to open each PDF to see what each document is. Not good.

- **Adopt the same practice for emails.** Use thoughtful and descriptive subject-matter lines in emails. Sometimes, an email stream will be forwarded on and on, and the topic of the email will change, but the subject line remains the same. Be the one who's proactive and changes the subject line of the email (but note in the body of the email that you changed the subject line). This makes it much easier for people to find emails going forward.

- **Acknowledge that you've received a communication.** When a partner emails or leaves you a voicemail, send a short email confirming receipt and noting that you're on it. This can be a three-word email: *"Thanks. On it,"* or *"Confirming receipt. Thanks."*

- **Ask for due dates and estimated time involved.** When getting a new assignment, always ask for the due date and an estimate of how much time the partner anticipates the project should take for you to complete it. Again, if you find yourself needing more time, communicate that to the partner as soon as possible, ideally well before the due date.

- **Don't ask the same question twice.** When you're working with partners, ask questions, but try not to ask the same question more than once. I think most partners appreciate getting questions from their associates. Partners recognize that they tend to speak in shorthand or at a higher level than an associate may be able to understand. But asking a partner the same question multiple times may indicate that you weren't paying attention the first time. If you don't understand something when the answer is first given to you, drill down immediately rather than going back later.

- **Be consistent and show up as your best self every day.** That will be harder to do on some days than others, but this is where you have to dig in and push harder. This is what it means to be a professional. Can you even imagine a firm partner telling a judge or a client on any given day that they're just not feeling it? It's the same for you as an associate. We're not supposed to be machines, but we do have to be professional. Difficult days can be expected, but instead of wishing for fewer hard times, work to make yourself better able to handle those times. In that vein, I strongly encourage you to take a few minutes to watch the video of Kara Lawson, the head coach of the Duke women's basketball team, speaking to her team about how, as they get older, they must get better at handling hard things. The talk named "Handle Hard Better" is available here: https://www.google.com/gasearch?q=handle%20hard% 20better&tbm=&source=sh/x/gs/ m2/5#fpstate=ive&vld=cid:e9d49db1,vid:oDzfZOfNki4,st:0

A Look Inside the Firm

"We're leaving for a ski trip in Utah tomorrow."

I had been working with a bright associate on an important case that was in active litigation. I really enjoyed working with him. We prepared a motion for summary judgment and agreed with our opposing counsel on the due date for their opposition papers. Our reply brief would be due five days after that. There were no surprises here as to the upcoming deadlines.

When the opposition brief came in, the associate and I had a long meeting to discuss our response. We talked about our strategies, the best arguments that we could make, and how to best position our legal arguments. I then asked if he could turn a draft around in three days, which would give me sufficient time to review it and get client approval. It was then that he announced for the first time that he was leaving in the morning for a ski trip in Utah. *What?*

I came to learn from other partners that this was his modus operandi. Despite his excellent legal skills and writing ability, I joined a list of partners who refused to work with him any longer due to his failure to take ownership of his matters.

Working with Difficult Partners

Unfortunately, not all partners are great to work with. There are some who you'll love working with. Others, however, are just the opposite. They may be distrustful, rude, disorganized, or have a reputation for deflecting responsibility and blaming others if things go wrong. If you find yourself working with a difficult partner, these tactical steps may help.

For particularly high-maintenance or distrustful partners, be proactive. Touch base while you're working on the assignment, just to say it's coming along well and that you're anticipating an on-time or even early completion, if that's true.

Promptly acknowledge all communication from the partner, even if just to say that you received them. Anticipate what the partner might need or want next. For example, if you receive a letter or a pleading in a matter, reach out to the partner before they reach out to you, and say that you're in the process of reviewing it and you'll provide a summary ASAP, or some other appropriate action. The point is don't wait to be told.

Partners who deflect responsibility and blame others are especially challenging to work with. They may be the type to say, "No one ever told me (this or that)," despite having been told before. Or "Why wasn't I asked about this before?" when, in fact, they were.

This may not be malicious on their part, but it can be stressful for people who have to work with them. In this type of circumstance, consider taking steps to create a record of your dealings with the partner. Maintain your written communications with the partner and keep them where you can easily find them.

Also, contemporaneously document your verbal communications. Don't do it in an accusatory way. Just write an email to yourself or a short memo to the file saying that you spoke with the partner on a specific date, or she instructed you to do a specific thing, or you informed them of specific information. Hopefully, it will never come to this, but at some point down the road, you may need that email or memo to politely remind the partner of that prior interaction.

If you're working for a disorganized partner, you can safely anticipate getting multiple requests for the same information or documents. If the partner asks for a paper copy of a document, make extra copies because you are likely to be asked for the same document again and again.

I once worked with a partner who routinely would ask me for copies of the same document. I learned to just make five copies: one to give him and the rest to keep handy for the four additional times he would ask for it.

Take Responsibility For Your Work, Including the Mistakes

Several years ago, I asked an associate to help me with a research project. Before he began his research, I pointed out one particular issue that was concerning to me. I asked him to pay special attention to it and explained why it was so important in our case.

When I received the associate's memo a few days later, I had serious doubts about his conclusions on the issue we'd discussed. I spent a few hours double-checking his research, and I saw that he got it wrong. I have to admit this really surprised me, given the discussion we had before he began the work.

When I met with the associate to explain why his conclusion was off base, his reaction was even worse than the mistake. Instead of saying, "Oh, I'm sorry I missed that," or "Thanks for walking me through the analysis," his comment was simply, "Do you want me to fix that?"

There was no apology. There was no acknowledgment of the lengthy discussions we'd had about the issue.

If you make a mistake, and we all do, take ownership of it. Apologize. Ask for feedback. Figure out how you got it wrong if it's not obvious. Then, of course, offer to redo the work.

Be a Good "Firm Citizen"

Law firms often keep lists, and they're not always good to be on. Firms keep track of hours, timeliness of billing entries, compliance with mandatory training requirements, work expenses, and more. Keep in mind that if you blow off these requirements, it becomes someone else's job, probably a partner you're trying to impress, to follow up with you. This does not make the partner's job easier or make you look good, despite the quality of your legal work.

Blowing off firm requirements can be a real reputation killer. Don't be the associate whose name frequents the firm's naughty lists. Consider these tips for becoming a good "firm citizen":

- **Learn the firm's document-management and billing systems.** Make sure you store documents, particularly case-related documents, correctly. Few things more frustrating than trying to locate an email or letter that has been filed under the wrong matter number. It's also important to make sure that you bill your time to the correct matter. Otherwise, the partner has to spend her time trying to figure out where your time entry belongs and moving it there.

- **Master legal technology.** Your ability to efficiently and effectively utilize the various legal research databases and e-discovery platforms that are available in today's legal market can keep unnecessary costs down, improve client relationships, and help you to stand out. Your inability to use those tools, on the other hand, can really limit the value that you can provide as an associate.

- **Be mindful of the firm's culture, values, and dress code.** Your desire for self-expression in your dress and language may have to take a backseat to the firm's culture, values, and dress code. I recently heard a story about a junior attorney who was asked not to wear her glittery sneakers in the workplace. Upon hearing this, she burst into tears, saying that she should be entitled to express herself at work— that this was her signature style. This was not well received. Remember, law firms are professional environments, and the culture and dress code are set by the firm.

- **Draft your time entries with care.** This prevents the partner from wasting time editing them for grammar and spelling errors or contacting you to provide additional details in your time descriptions.

- **Don't act inappropriately at firm parties, retreats, or client events.** Everyone knows of an associate, and sometimes a partner, who drank too much at a firm event and engaged in highly embarrassing, offensive, or even actionable conduct. You really don't want to be that guy. For some, especially associates, it can be the end of your job at the firm.

- **Enter your time every day, or you'll likely end up losing time.** Or worse, your time entries may become somewhat fictional. Firms often monitor who is entering their time on a daily basis, and you don't want to be "reminded" to do what you're expected to do.

- **Do not write off your own time.** However, always use common sense about what you put on a client bill. For example, if the managing partner of your office asks all the associates to prepare a list and short description of their assigned matters, do not bill that time to the client.

- **Learn to discipline yourself.** When it comes to complying with firm mandates and respecting the firm's culture and values, monitor yourself so others don't need to discipline you.

Things they don't teach you in law school

I have seen many associates (and some partners) damage their reputations and even derail their careers by talking too much, failing to control their emotions, and being the kind of person that people don't want to work with. Typically, these pitfalls are entirely avoidable. I've also seen many associates become highly regarded and sought after because they exercise good judgment, stay out of trouble, and are easy to work with.

Here are some key tips to help you succeed as a law firm associate. This is nuts and bolts advice, the things you likely did not hear about in law school that can make or break your legal career.

- **Don't gossip.** When you're going into a new workplace, remember that the person who gossips to you will also likely gossip about you. This was the best piece of advice my mom gave me when I first started working in a professional setting. Do your best not to engage in gossip. Keep in mind that once you say something or send that email with "gossipy" content, you lose control over those words, but you still remain responsible for them.

- **Be nice to everyone in the firm.** You should be respectful to everyone you work with, no matter what their position is, because it's the right thing to do, but also because your job may depend on it. One of the associates in my starting associate class quickly got a reputation for being condescending to the firm's legal assistants. He was quietly terminated in just a few months, even though his work was good, and he acted appropriately to other attorneys. I remember him telling me on one occasion, "She's just a staff member," when I asked him why he spoke rudely to someone in the firm. In my experience, this type of behavior is never tolerated, even from the most talented attorneys. And if doing the right thing isn't enough motivation for you, keep in mind that legal assistants, receptionists, and other staff members often have the ear of the most senior people in the law firm. If you need even more motivation, imagine being the associate who had to explain why he was terminated from his first law firm job after just two months.

- **Use discretion about what you share about your personal life.** I can think of countless times over the course of my career when information that was shared in confidence with one "trusted" attorney became well-known throughout the law firm. I'm not saying to never discuss personal matters with someone at the firm, just be very careful about the people with whom you share that information. And if someone confides in you about a personal matter, don't make them regret their decision to trust you.

- **Don't become your emotions.** Avoid outbursts and other public displays of emotion. I recognize that we're all human, but consider the time and place before reacting in an overly emotional manner. Your circumstances simply cannot dictate your emotions, especially in a professional workplace. Just one temper tantrum can do serious damage to how you are viewed by your colleagues. It will raise questions about your professionalism and judgment, and it may even risk your career.

- **Keep in mind that partners talk to each other.** A lot. Many partners have a long history of knowing and working with each other, even if they're not in the same practice, group, or office. If you do great work for one partner but not for another, it will be discussed. If you try to play one partner off another partner, you likely will be exposed. If you have a way of getting over or manipulating one partner, other partners will notice, and it will not serve you well.

- **Deal well with criticism.** Criticism and negative feedback are inevitable in life, and lawyers, like everyone else, must be able to respond appropriately. Even if someone's criticism of you is delivered poorly or in an unartful way, you still should ask yourself, "Is there some truth to this? Is there a kernel of truth in what is being said to me, even though it's being said in a nasty way by somebody who I don't like or appreciate?" Don't make matters worse by getting emotional in your response to the criticism. Instead, keep your cool, ask questions, and try to get to the bottom of it. It may be an area where you have a blind spot or an area where you can make real improvements. However, if you think the criticism is not justified, keep your cool and ask for help in understanding the basis of the criticism. You can subtly make your point that the criticism is off base by saying something like: This is what happened, this is what I did, how should I have handled it differently, what would you have done? In that way, you'll be able to make your case that you did act appropriately, and that the criticism isn't deserved.

- **Thrive in challenging situations.** Things will go wrong despite your best efforts. And you will make mistakes. How you handle these situations will make all the difference in how well you emerge from them. When you're dealing with a negative situation, no matter what the cause, don't get emotional, catastrophize, or simply blow it off. Instead, I recommend that you practice neutral thinking. The late Trevor Moawad, author of *It Takes What It Takes*, described neutral thinking as a high-performance strategy that emphasizes judgment-free thinking, especially in crises and pressure situations. It's not positive thinking, but it's definitely not negative thinking. Instead, it forces you to take a pragmatic approach to any situation and ask, *What's one thing I can do to improve the situation?* Give yourself a minute for your brain to process that question, and you may be surprised at how resourceful you may be in coming up with a good answer. But if you're having trouble, pretend you are a high-performance coach working with a client who is having that exact same problem. What would your advice to that person be?

- **Remember that you, for the most part, are in control of your reputation.** With that in mind, ask yourself, *Who do I want to be? How do I want to be seen in the workplace?* What three words do you want your colleagues to use to describe you? What three words would you hate for your colleagues to use to describe you? Keep your reputation top of mind throughout your entire career. It's true that it can take years to build a good reputation, but only one minute to destroy it. It's hard to undo a bad reputation, so guard your good reputation with diligence.

- **Focus on the Long Game.** Always remember that strong associates get better assignments. They get more responsibility. And then they get client-facing opportunities that ease their path to partnership. Despite any daily annoyances or frustrations, always remember that you're playing the long game.

- **Take ownership of your professional development.** You should constantly study legal developments in your practice area without being told to do so, even if you're not dealing with that precise issue on any of your matters. This is a great way to build your reputation and eventually demonstrate that you're partnership material. Plus, you never know when a partner or client may have a need for the expertise you've developed.

- **Don't sabotage your reputation and credibility by turning in sloppy work.** An occasional typo here and there can be expected, but handing in work products filled with typos, poor formatting, incorrect case sites, and very bad grammar is simply not acceptable. Take the time to proofread your work carefully. After you've completed a draft, consider putting it down for a few minutes and going for a walk, or getting another change of scenery. Clear your head, think about something else, and then come back to your document with fresh eyes. Sometimes just sitting in a different chair when you review your work can help you to review it more effectively.

- **Focus on time management.** It's very hard for associates to control their own time, which makes it even more important to have a plan going each day for the work you're going to prioritize. Put those projects on your schedule. If it's important to you, it should be on your schedule.

- **Stay in Touch with Your Network.** Stay in touch with your law school friends and former colleagues. Very few people understand the pressures lawyers face and the dynamics of law firm life. But if you maintain a solid network of friends in the legal industry, you will always have people to turn to who have been there and done that, and can offer advice and support to help you navigate challenges in your career. They can also become a referral network for business, and some of them may even become clients.

- **Stand Out from the Crowd.** One of the best things I did during my career as an associate was to be at the office by 6:00 a.m. every morning. I know you're thinking that it is absolutely insane, and maybe it was. At first, I did it only to beat the traffic and HOV restrictions during my morning commute. But I soon found out that having those three hours that I myself could completely control launched my career to a whole new level. That time was golden. No one was calling, emailing, or dropping by my office to interrupt me.

I had three hours of quiet time, during which I could intensely focus on my work. And man, did I get things done. My reputation as a dedicated associate went through the roof, and I kept getting better and more high-profile cases to work on, including a matter that went to trial for ten weeks!

Special Opportunities to Grow

Some firms provide additional opportunities that can provide associates with exceptional opportunities to learn and grow. These can include secondments and mentoring programs. Seriously consider taking advantage of these opportunities if they're available to you.

- **Secondments**

In case you're not familiar with the term, a secondment is an agreement between a law firm and one of its clients whereby an attorney, seconded from the law firm, goes to work for the client, typically in their legal department, for a set period of time.

A secondment may be full-time or part-time, and the firm may or may not receive compensation for the secondee's work. A secondment can be a great way to see the other side of client relationships. You put yourself in the shoes of your clients and understand how their world works, the pressures and responsibilities they have, and how they think about and deal with outside counsel like you.

This can be an invaluable experience when you head back to your law firm. You will know from first-hand experience exactly what your client needs and why. It's also a great opportunity to build your personal and your firm's relationship with your client. If your firm offers secondment opportunities, I will strongly recommend that you look into that, especially as a junior lawyer.

Over the years, many of my partner colleagues were seconded to clients early in their careers, and they took advantage of the opportunity to build long-term relationships that have been incredibly beneficial to their career growth and business development. Plus, they often made friends for life.

- **Leverage Mentors and Sponsors**

Sign up for a mentor if your firm has a formal mentoring program. But regardless of whether or not your firm has a formal program, in my experience, mentor or sponsor relationships that are organically developed are the best.

To find a mentor or a sponsor at a law firm, you need to actively engage in networking events, participate in firm-sponsored activities, and seek out opportunities to connect with senior professionals at your firm. Express your interest in mentorship to colleagues and superiors, and demonstrate your commitment to learning and growth.

Building genuine relationships within the firm can increase your chances of finding a sponsor or mentor who aligns with your career goals. You may not work directly for your mentor, and they may not even be a partner. Senior associates who know the firm and the ins and outs of practice, and who are not very far removed from being in your exact situation, can be great mentors.

A mentor can provide guidance and advice and share their experiences to help you navigate your career so you can best position yourself for partnership. Here are some ways a good mentor can help you:

- **Goal setting:** A mentor can assist in setting realistic short-term and long-term goals aligned with your career aspirations and the firm's partnership criteria.

- **Feedback and improvement:** Mentors can provide ongoing feedback on your performance, highlighting strengths and areas for improvement. This constructive input aids in continuous professional development.

- **Client-relationship guidance:** For associates involved in client interactions, mentors can offer great advice on building and managing client relationships effectively, an absolutely critical aspect for partnership consideration.

- **Visibility and recognition:** Mentors guide associates on how to gain visibility within the firm, such as presenting at internal meetings, contributing to thought leadership, or participating in firm committees.

- **Mental toughness:** Your journey to partnership can be demanding. Mentors can offer support and guidance on maintaining mental toughness, resilience, and a positive mindset amid challenges.

- **Advocacy, but in a different way:** While mentors may not have the same clout and decision-making power as sponsors, they can still speak positively about your achievements and potential when asked for input during partnership evaluations and during associate reviews.

- **Ethical and professional standards:** Mentors should emphasize the importance of upholding ethical and professional standards—vital qualities for anybody who aspires to be a partner in a law firm. You can also turn to a mentor if you are put in an ethically challenging position by another partner.

- **Succession planning:** Mentors can help associates think strategically about succession planning and position them to take on leadership roles as more senior partners transition or retire.

- **Cross-firm exposure:** Mentors may encourage associates to explore opportunities in different practice areas or departments within the firm. That broadens your experience and makes you a more versatile candidate for partnerships. It also introduces you to more partners throughout your firm. This can be especially valuable if you work for a large law firm.

- **Crisis management and challenging situations:** Mentors can offer advice on crisis management, which can help an associate demonstrate their ability to handle high-pressure situations effectively. By providing holistic guidance and support, mentors can contribute to your overall professional development, help you navigate the complexities of law firm dynamics, and position yourself for success on the path to partnership.

- **Find a Go-To Sponsor**

A sponsor, on the other hand, is different from a mentor. In my experience, a sponsor is someone who you have worked directly with and who will leverage their influence and relationships to promote your professional development and promotion within the firm.

A sponsor will actively advocate for your career advancement, help secure high-profile assignments, and support your progression within the firm. A sponsor who knows you well can stand up for you if you and your reputation are under attack, and when you're ready, will encourage other partners to vote for you when you're up for partnership.

Moving On? Keep It Classy

There may be a hundred reasons why you decide to leave your law firm. You may be dissatisfied there. You may be moving to a different location. You may want to change your focus. You may want more money. You may not like the people you work with.

Regardless of your reason for wanting to leave the law firm, resigning from the firm is a significant professional step.

Even though the days of one person staying at a law firm for life are long gone, you should make this decision in a very reasoned way. Here are a few suggested approaches you can take to resign gracefully from your law firm:

- **Offer your resignation in person.** Schedule a meeting with your immediate supervisor, or other appropriate people at your firm to discuss your resignation. Don't tell your friends in the law firm first because, as I noted above, anything you say can, and probably will, be shared, and you don't want firm leadership to first hear about your resignation from somebody else.

- **Prepare a formal resignation letter.** Indicate your last working day, bearing in mind that you should offer at least two weeks' notice. Keep the letter concise, professional, and positive. Express gratitude for the opportunities and experiences you gained at the firm.

- **Be prepared to explain why you're leaving.** Focus on the positive aspects of your decision, such as new opportunities for professional growth or career development. I would avoid using this as an opportunity to vent grievances. Remember, it's a small world, and you must protect your reputation at all times. The last thing you want is for people to say, "Well, we really never liked him or her anyway."

- **Offer assistance in your transition.** Express your willingness to assist in a smooth transition on the matters you're working on. Offer to train a successor, prepare case summaries, and transfer memos, or provide any necessary handover support.

- **Be prepared to discuss an appropriate notice period.** This may vary based on your position, the firm's policies, and the matters you're working on. Leaving a firm in the lurch on the eve of trial, or at some other significant time, will not do anything to enhance your professional reputation.

- **Always maintain professionalism.** Keep the conversation professional, avoid negative comments about the firm, colleagues, or clients. Focus on positive experiences and the learning you gained from them.

- **Work diligently to complete pending tasks and projects before your departure.** Leaving your colleagues in the lurch by not finishing work you've started could damage the good reputation you've taken time to build. And you never know when your path may cross again with your soon-to-be former colleagues.

- **Say goodbye graciously.** Consider sending out a group email to the firm or to the team you work with, thanking them for the opportunity and providing your new contact information, if you would like. Try to foster positive relationships and leave a good final impression.

- **Follow up after the resignation.** After you have your meeting with your supervisor, follow up with an email to reiterate your gratitude, your agreed last working day, and any additional details you discussed at the meeting. Remember, professionalism and courtesy are key during the resignation process. Leaving on good terms can actually enhance your professional brand and potential future references.

- **Do your best to leave on good terms.** Always remember that years from now, if you're applying for another job or for admission to another state bar, you'll likely be asked to provide references from every law firm job you've had.

- **Don't be a "job hopper."** Although you may not stay at one law firm for your entire career, you don't want to get a reputation for being a "job hopper." You may have to gut it out at a firm you don't love for longer than you'd otherwise like before making a move. You'll have to explain every move you've made in your career when you're interviewing in the future, so make sure you have a positive story to tell.

When It's Not Your Choice to Leave

If you have been fired or laid off from your associate position, resist the urge to go on a social media rant about how terrible the firm is and how unfairly you were treated, even if it's true.

Never forget that your reputation is your most important asset, and potential employers may hear about your post or find it during their pre-interview research about you, and may then be reluctant to hire you.

Instead, ask yourself, *What's my next best move in integrity? What's the opportunity here?* This will put you in a more resourceful mindset and get you thinking about future possibilities. And always ask what lessons you can learn from this experience.

Action Steps

- Remember that partners will always seek out associates who are competent, positive, Reliable, and easy to work with. Make sure that you can check those boxes.

- Being a good "firm citizen" can be just as important as doing great legal work. Stay off the firm's naughty lists, and never create problems that the partners you're trying to impress have to deal with.

CHAPTER 3

Become Their Next Partner

How can I be seen as partnership material?

Are you ready?

Over the years, the most common reason why associates are not promoted to partnership is because he or she is just not ready. This may be due to requirements outside the associate's control. For example, the firm may have minimum requirements, perhaps eight years, concerning how long the associate has been practicing law, or how many years the associate has been with the firm. In any given year, the firm also may not be in a financial position to promote associates to partnership.

But putting issues like that aside, there are countless things an associate can do to increase their chances of being promoted—things that are entirely in the associate's control. The table stake, of course, is doing great legal work.

Assuming you've got that handled when you throw your hat into the ring for partnership, there are key qualities the firm expects you to have and show the potential to achieve. Here's a summary of the key factors that go into the mix:

- **Demonstrate maturity.** One way to do this is by being a problem solver, not a problem bringer. Always present a potential solution or two when calling the firm partners' attention to a problem. This reduces their cognitive load, which leaders always appreciate, and helps position you as someone with an ownership mentality. For example, if the firm is having trouble with associate retention, do some research and present a realistic plan for the partners' consideration to address the problem.

- **Develop a deep understanding of your work.** Learn the business of law, the business of your firm, and the business of your firm's clients.

- **Be a reliably good "firm citizen."** You should also have a great track record of good firm citizenship, especially in terms of getting your time in, having good time entries, serving on firm committees, and demonstrating an ownership mentality.

On the other hand, any of these issues may *negatively* impact your chances of promotion:

- You don't hit your billable-hour requirements.
- You have to be chased to get your time in.
- Your time entries have to be heavily edited.
- You haven't run any cases from beginning to end with only minimal oversight from a partner.
- You've worked with only a few partners at the firm, and the other partners don't otherwise know you.
- You haven't demonstrated a commitment to the firm by doing the unrequired, even if you meet your billable requirements. You're known for doing the bare minimum and nothing more.
- You have a reputation for being a gossiper or troublemaker.
- You haven't delegated or supervised the work of junior attorneys.

- You don't have a strong sponsor, or support from current partners.
- You don't act like a partner. You haven't demonstrated an ownership mentality, including building client relationships, looking for business-development opportunities, following firm procedures, and presenting solutions to problems.

The good news is that these issues generally are 100 percent in your control. That means that you alone can fix them.

Get on the Radar of Other Firm Partners

If you don't know enough partners, consider going to firm events and meeting as many partners as you can. If that's not feasible, ask an influential partner who you have a relationship with to introduce you to other partners in the firm. This can be done virtually or in person.

Those new introductions may not lead to an actual sponsorship for your partnership, but you may at least get some support from the people you meet, who may offer a positive opinion on your bid for promotion. Keep in mind that when a partner asks other partners to take those types of meetings, those asks are almost always agreed to. Partners always like to accommodate requests from other partners.

Aside from in-person meetings, connect with the firm partners on LinkedIn, and like or share their content. Serve on firm committees, and mentor junior partners.

Some things, however, may not be in your control, such as working with lots of different partners and getting good experience with things like depositions, trials, and client meetings. If you find yourself not getting those good experiences, it's your chance to be proactive and ask what you can do to get those types of experiences in advance. This alone can demonstrate the type of initiative that shows you are partnership material.

Act as if You Are Already a Partner

During an interview for partnership, a candidate said: "I have amazing connections I can develop if I get promoted. I can also make great introductions for other partners." He obviously thought this would make him look ready for the job. Unfortunately, my other partners and I wondered why he hadn't already done those things. Consider how much more credibility he would have had and how much more powerful his pitch would have been if he had shown initiative, acted with an ownership mentality, and already taken those steps. This is when acting as if you're already a partner would have helped.

Think and Plan in Advance

Applying for partnership is not something that you should do lightly, and certainly not something you should do simply because you've been at the firm or practiced law for the minimum number of years required. Instead, it takes thoughtful and advanced planning.

At least two years before applying for a promotion, start thinking about how you can put yourself in the best position to succeed. Talk to trusted partners and ask them for their suggestions about how to best position yourself for partnership. Ask them directly if they think you should make that move now or perhaps wait a year or two.

You also should start formulating a business-development plan that focuses on key clients and relationships. Consider ways that you can bring in new clients and strengthen relationships with existing clients. Perhaps you can develop expertise in a new area of law that will serve the interests of your firm's clients, or you can introduce partners to potential new clients. Be ready to present your plan verbally to the partnership if you have the opportunity.

Become Involved

You may also want to volunteer for leadership on firm committees, such as associate or mentor committees. Look for opportunities that will add the most value to the firm and highlight your unique gifts and strengths.

Being involved in relevant industry groups, bar associations, and civic activities also may help your case for partnership. Writing articles, speaking at conferences, and developing your reputation as a go-to person in your area of the law also helps.

Prepare for Your Presentations

If your firm requires you to make some type of formal presentation in connection with your bid for partnership, plan it out way in advance and practice, practice, practice. If it's a virtual presentation, practice getting on the platform, sharing your screen, pulling up your PowerPoint if you're using one, and putting it in presentation mode.

Videotape yourself and watch it back, as painful as it may be, and look for ways to improve. Anticipate the types of questions you may receive, and prepare solid answers for them. Ask some trusted colleagues if you can do a mock presentation for them to practice. And closely consider any feedback you get.

If You Don't Get the Promotion. . .

Although it may not be held against you if you fail in your first partnership election, it's probably best to wait until you know you're ready before applying for partnership. This is when your relationships with key partners, mentors, and sponsors really come into play. Ask for their honest assessments concerning your readiness to go through the process. And if they don't feel you're ready, take their advice on how to get ready.

Before You Become a Partner. . .

Becoming a partner is a business decision, not an ego decision. Before taking that leap, it's crucial to understand the contractual obligations that you may be undertaking, particularly with an equity partnership. At the outset, I would strongly encourage you to ensure that the firm is committed to your specific practice area before you sign on the dotted line.

Years ago, I was working on some massive matters in which our clients were averse to companies in a specific industry sector. These were very lucrative cases for my law firm. Nevertheless, another more senior and influential partner at the firm wanted to target that same industry sector for his line of work. The managing partner met with me, asking if I could switch sides in my practice area so he could accommodate the request from the other partner. This, of course, would not work for me.

Fortunately, I had a very large and portable book of business and was able to move on to another firm right away. The same thing has happened to other friends and colleagues over the years. You can't always predict these things. After all, they are business decisions based on market trends and other factors. But do your best to confirm that the firm is committed to your area of practice before you make a partnership commitment, which complicates any future lateral moves.

Confirm How Partners are Compensated

Don't forget about the impact on your personal finances if you become a firm partner, particularly an equity partner. Speak to the finance people at your firm concerning exactly how—not just how much—partners are compensated. Is there a required equity contribution? Does the firm finance that contribution? What are the details around that? What is the repayment schedule? What if you decide to leave the firm before you have repaid? Are taxes withheld from partner distributions?

In how many states will I have to file tax returns? Will I have to pay 100 percent of my medical benefits and other perks when I'm a partner? Inquire into the financial health of the firm before you take on the responsibility of equity partnership, where a regular paycheck is not guaranteed.

Is the firm overleveraged? Is the firm able to manage its debt? What type of real-estate commitments does the firm have? I frequently get emails from headhunters trying to gauge my interest in moving to another firm. Sometimes, the headhunter says the firm is willing to overpay for the right lateral partner. To me, this is a major red flag. I would not want to go to a firm that overpays its partners. We've all heard about firms that overleveraged themselves to attract high-profile lateral partners and found themselves bankrupt, with firm partners personally on the hook for the firm's debt.

Hire an Accountant

Prepare to hire a good accountant with law partner experience to help you navigate the financial implications of being a law firm partner. Don't become one of the partners who didn't realize that taxes were not being withheld from their partner distributions, and bought fancy new cars or went on vacation with money that actually belonged to Uncle Sam.

Some partners are actually shocked when they find out that partner distributions are sometimes missed and can vary widely in amount. A good accountant or financial adviser can help you budget for such contingencies.

Partnership Planning Strategy

If your goal is to become a partner, I would advise that you develop an action plan to put yourself in the best position to succeed. Doing great legal work is table stakes, of course. But the following areas can be just as important to helping you achieve your partnership goal.

- **Model Successful Partners**

Look around your law firm and identify the most successful partners. Try to figure out what they do to stand out. How are they different? What makes them special? What are they doing to develop business? What are their daily habits? What energy do they bring to the office, to meetings, and when they go to court? How do they maintain relationships with their existing clients? How have they built their reputation in and outside of the firm?

I have never worked with a successful partner who was a complainer or negative. Instead, they're growth-minded action-takers, and they're not waiting for anyone to hand them anything. They are internally motivated and driven to succeed. And, frankly, they do get frustrated by partners who don't take initiative to bring in their own business but expect introductions to potential clients and to be fed business brought in by the rock-star partners.

Take every opportunity you can to work directly with one of your firm's standout partners. Watch how they manage their time, how they interact with clients, opposing counsel, judges, associates, staff, and their partners. Learn from their habits and adopt them. Be yourself, but don't reinvent the wheel. Learn from and model the best.

- **Look and Act the Part**

A key way to be thought of as a potential partner is to start looking and acting like a partner before you're promoted. Here are some key areas to focus on:

1. **Confidence**

   Confidence is key to having a partnership presence. It's about believing in yourself and your abilities. Practice confident body language—standing tall, maintaining eye contact, and using a firm handshake.

   Unquestionably, confidence also comes from being prepared. Ensure that you're on top of all the relevant facts and issues in your matters so you'll be ready to handle any questions or challenges that may come up.

2. **Professionalism**

   Even in a business-casual environment, it's important to strike the right balance between professionalism and comfort. Choose clothes that are appropriate for a business-casual setting but still convey professionalism. Don't wear wrinkled or poorly fitting clothes, and make sure your shoes are polished. Avoid clothing that is too casual or revealing.

3. **Communication Skills**

   Effective communication is essential to maintaining a partnership presence. Speak clearly and confidently, and avoid upspeak (a rising intonation that sounds like a question), which can make you sound less confident. And listen more than you speak.

4. **Active Listening**

Active listening involves fully engaging with the speaker and demonstrating that you understand their perspective, even if you don't agree with it. This means making eye contact, nodding in agreement or acknowledgment, and asking for clarification when necessary.

Avoid interrupting and genuinely consider the speaker's point of view before responding. Don't be the person who doesn't actually hear anything other people are saying and is simply waiting for a pause in the discussion so they can start talking.

5. **Body Language**

Your body language can speak volumes about your confidence and professionalism. Maintain good posture, avoid slouching or crossing your arms, and use gestures to emphasize your points. Be mindful of your facial expressions, which can convey a lot of information about your attitude and emotions, even if you don't realize it. By all means, avoid distracting personal ticks, like hair twirling and nail-biting.

6. **Adaptability**

A partnership presence also involves being able to adapt well to different or unexpected situations. One predictable thing about being a law firm partner is that you never know what may happen at your firm or in your matters. The most impressive partners are those who handle unexpected situations with an air of confidence, competence, and grace.

7. **Relationships**

Building relationships is a critical aspect of a solid partnership presence. Take the time to network with colleagues, clients, and other lawyers. Be approachable, show genuine interest in others, and look for opportunities to connect and collaborate. I've never met a successful partner who doesn't have great people skills and can't interact well with others. The most impressive partners have deep networks of trusted colleagues and friends.

8. **Leadership**

Partnership presence requires demonstrating leadership qualities, even if you're not in a formal leadership role. Take initiative, offer solutions to problems, and inspire others with your vision and ideas. Show confidence in your abilities, and be willing to take on challenges and lead by example.

Evaluate whether you have a partnership presence. Can you effectively command attention and respect in your firm? Work on developing these traits to position yourself well for partnership.

- **Master Networking**

I'm sure you've noticed that a familiar theme throughout this book is the importance of connecting with people, oftentimes people you don't know, in order to build a successful legal career. Some people, however, would rather get a root canal than attend a professional networking event, especially if they don't know anybody there.

I encourage you to push through your apprehension and approach these opportunities by looking for ways you can *give* and not *get*, and focusing on how to be more *interested* than *interesting*. In my view this is an essential skill to becoming and succeeding as a partner.

A Look Inside the Firm

"This is ridiculous."

Seemingly insignificant interactions can present an opportunity that can make a huge difference in your career growth as well as your job satisfaction. Here's one of my favorite examples of that.

I was retained to represent a client in a major case in Texas. I remember going to my first defense counsel meeting in a beautiful office building in Houston. When I arrived at the law firm hosting the meeting, the receptionist pointed me toward a large conference room with a closed door. As I opened the door and walked in, I saw a room full of guys, and I do mean *guys*, sitting around the conference room table, fully engaged in conversation, laughing, and generally having a good time as they were waiting for the meeting to start.

I quickly realized I was the only woman, and I think they did too. They all stood up, said hi, and were super friendly. I went around the room and introduced myself to each person, and then I found an empty seat at the table and started to settle in. I guess it kind of threw them that I was there because all the conversation that had been going on when I showed up had completely stopped.

We all sat there in an awkward silence. I could have buried my face in my phone as I waited for the meeting to start, but instead, I said to myself, *This is ridiculous!* before asking a seven-word question that changed everything.

"Did anyone see that game last night?"

Well, you would have thought Oprah walked in the room and gave everyone a car. The room erupted with discussion about the game, and I eventually made relationships that I still have to this day. I also became the lead counsel of the defense group. . . all from choosing to say seven words to people I didn't know.

Action Steps

- Closely observe and model the behavior of the most successful partners at your firm.

- Don't wait to become a partner to start acting like a partner.

- Your promotion will depend in large part on the people you know at your firm, so make yourself a known quantity to your firm's partners.

CHAPTER 4

Be a Successful Partner

*How do I show appreciation for my clients
and make their lives easier?*

Yes, in many ways, you're a salesperson.

I was a first-year lawyer at my very first law firm. I remember walking into the firm's largest conference room for a meeting with all the junior partners and associates. It was a business-development meeting. The firm had hired a marketing specialist to come in and meet with us. I sat next to a junior partner with whom I had been working, and she was muttering under her breath, "I didn't go to law school to become a salesperson."

That was over thirty years ago, but it's shocking to me how many attorneys still go into law firm practice with that mindset. They seem to think that cases will just somehow appear on their desks. I can assure you that is not the case.

In my experience, there are two different types of partners: Those with their own book of business are rainmakers, and those who work on matters brought in by other partners are often referred to as service partners. Many partners start out as service partners but then develop their own book of business. Both rainmakers and service partners can have long, successful careers, but my preference was to become a rainmaker. There are a lot of reasons you should consider going that route, too.

The Importance of Being a Rainmaker

In many firms, there is an expectation, or even a requirement, that partners develop their own book of business. But putting that issue aside, having your own book of business is, in my view, the best (and perhaps only) way to control your own future, have some degree of autonomy, as well as have a say in how the firm operates. It also gives you freedom to move to another law firm, if you'd like, and undoubtedly gives you the opportunity to make a lot more money. In many ways, "rainmakers" control their own fate by taking responsibility for building and retaining client relationships, scaling their practices by developing teams of associates and ensuring quality work.

Although service partners may also have direct client engagement, they likely are not the owner of the relationship, and they typically do not retain ultimate responsibility for it. But that doesn't mean "service partners" don't have clients.

Basically, the rainmaker is their client. Smart service partners treat the rainmakers like a client, with a goal of making the rainmaker's job easier.

Being a service partner is not without risk, however. What if the rainmaker decides to start assigning work to other partners? What if the rainmaker leaves the firm along with all the business you've been working on?

Service partners should be aware of the risks of being entirely dependent on only one rainmaker for their entire workload and should consider developing relationships with other partners who can become a source of work as well.

In my view, however, every partner should take ownership over their own career and remember that no one, including their partners, owes them anything. Work *on* your business, not just *in* your or another partner's business.

This means putting yourself out there to develop client relationships and a sustainable book of business. When you build strong client relationships over time, your clients will trust you and stick with you through both the good times and the bad.

I learned this lesson in a huge way when I was a third-year associate. I was part of a trial team led by Dave, a senior partner with a rock-solid reputation and long-term industry relationships. We were brought in to try a case after the firm that had been handling the matter could no longer serve in that role. We flew off to a small county in rural Wisconsin to take over the case on the eve of trial.

Following a contentious two-week trial, the jury announced that they'd reached a verdict. We sat at the counsel table, along with our client, and listened as the jury foreman stood up and announced the decision. The plaintiff was awarded even more money than they had asked for! As counsel for the defendant, we were shell-shocked.

As I walked out of the courtroom with the client, the man who had to report this to his supervisors turned to me and said, "Thank God we had Dave. I don't know what would have happened if we didn't have Dave."

Even after news of the verdict had reached the client's home office, no one questioned Dave's ability, judgment, or trial skills. The client knew they had the right guy for the case and stuck with him through the duration. By the way, that trust was not misplaced. Led by Dave, we got a complete reversal on appeal.

Look to Give, Not to Get

As you're working to develop your own client relationships, perhaps at a conference or networking event, don't go into the event focused on yourself. Instead of feeling uncomfortable, look for ways to make other people more comfortable. Strike up a conversation with someone who is by himself. Be more interested than interesting by asking him where he's from and what he thinks of the conference so far.

Look for ways you can offer assistance to people you meet. Smile, be friendly, put your phone in your pocket, and look to add value to everyone you meet.

Take the pressure off yourself by realizing that no one expects you to meet an ideal client who hires you for a major case on the spot at a networking event!

Proactive Patience - Process over Results

Developing a book of business typically does not happen overnight. You may have strong relationships with ideal clients, but it still may be years before they have a matter to send you. This is where the importance of proactive patience comes into play. This means consistently doing the things you need to do to develop your business, even though you're not seeing immediate results.

I was working with a young associate at my firm on a matter involving a cutting-edge area of the law at that time. The issue involved whether a company that got sued for making robocalls and sending junk faxes was entitled to insurance coverage. We realized there were no good articles on the subject, so we decided to write one ourselves.

In terms of legal content, the article was terrific. But it was a bit dry, to say the least! When we were just about to finalize it, the associate said he had a great idea. "Let's add the name of this new hit song to the title of the article. We can name it 'Call Me Maybe!'"

I had never heard of the song, but it sounded great to me. We added that to the title, and the article went about as viral as any insurance article could possibly go. Hundreds and hundreds of people commented on it and liked it, yet we got no work from it for months.

But I didn't sit there and say, "Oh well. I guess all this article-writing and content-marketing doesn't really work." Instead, I kept going. I keep generating content consistently, week after week.

One day, about eighteen months after the article had been published, I got a phone call. It was the head of claims at a large insurance company, which had their first robocall matter. She asked the law firms she typically worked with if they could assist, but they never even heard of the issue. So, she googled it and found the famous "Call Me Maybe" article.

This led to what has become one of my most treasured client relationships, which is still going to this day.

Be Cognizant of the Stress Your Clients are Under

As an associate, your job in large part was to make the partners' lives easier. As a partner, your job in large part is to make your clients' lives easier. A key part of doing that is to understand your clients' responsibilities, which likely include legal spend, budgeting, reporting to management, and assessing the likely outcome of their matters. Look for ways to take pressure off your clients by anticipating their needs and doing your best to alleviate their stress.

A Look Inside the Firm

"I would have been a wreck!"

My client had just signed the settlement agreement, resolving what had been a very contentious litigation. Opposing counsel had continuously accused my client of acting in bad faith, which was dead wrong. But those types of allegations impacted my client on a personal level because he was extremely ethical and diligent in his job.

Throughout the matter, the lawyer on the other side routinely sent emails on Friday nights around midnight, attaching snarly letters—your classic nasty gram—apparently designed to ruin everybody's weekend. Fortunately, we were eventually able to resolve the matter, and we did achieve a great financial outcome, but for me, the most important thing was my client saying that I had kept him calm throughout the unnecessary drama caused by the belligerent lawyer on the other side and that he would have been a wreck otherwise.

Be cognizant of the stresses your clients are under, including the fact that they, too, have reporting requirements in their organizations. Recognize that the client's reputation could be on the line if you don't do a good job. Keeping your clients' interests top of mind will make clients trust you even more and want to work with you more on a going-forward basis.

Value Every Client

Value each and every client opportunity you have been given. And don't allow yourself to be perceived as a fungible lawyer or someone who simply handles matters in a transactional way. Someone like that can be easily replaced!

Clients can hire any lawyer to do the work, but you have to be the lawyer they want to work with. Out of all the lawyers in the world, they chose you to work on that given matter.

Build Real Relationships

Whenever possible, build personal relationships with your clients. Show them you care about them. If they mention their birthday or their kids' names, write that down. Remember their favorite sports teams, or their most-hated sports teams! Look for ways to bond on a human level.

Help Your Clients Do Their Jobs

Something that I religiously do is look for ways that I can reach out to clients at unexpected times to add value and help them do their jobs better.

For example, I forward articles of professional, or even personal, interest and proactively alert them to new developments in the law that may impact their industry and ability to do their jobs. I try to see around the corner as to what's happening next in their area and then advise them.

To do this, I conduct research every morning—seven days a week—for new developments, regulations, and cases in cybersecurity, privacy, and insurance that I can alert my clients to and post on LinkedIn. This has been invaluable in strengthening and developing client relationships, as well as my personal brand and reputation as someone with a finger on the pulse of my industry.

Another thing you can do is offer assistance when your clients are seeking candidates for open positions. I recently helped a client who was unhappy at his current job by introducing him to another client who was trying to fill a senior role on his team. He ended up getting the job, and it turned out to be a perfect win-win.

A Look Inside the Firm

"I knew you would cry, but I know you'll love it forever."

A few years ago, I was working with a new client. During some personal chitchat, as we got to know each other, I mentioned that my dog, Cubby, had recently finished chemotherapy for lymphoma and was in remission.

My client was also a dog lover, and we traded pictures and stories about our little pups. Unfortunately, Cubby's lymphoma soon relapsed, and she passed away just a few weeks later. I was crushed.

A couple of weeks after that, I received a package with my client's return address. When she had asked for my address a couple of weeks before, I thought she was sending a card or note to acknowledge Cubby's passing, so I had no idea what could be in this box.

I opened it to find a spectacular portrait of Cubby that my client had made from one of the pictures I'd sent her. I have to admit that I was a bit emotional when I saw it. When I got myself together enough to call and thank her, she said she knew I would cry, but that I would love it for my entire life. She was right about that.

But her tremendously thoughtful gesture also indicated that she valued our relationship and the work we did together.

Think about things that you can do to show your clients that you truly care about them. Send a birthday card or note. Send a get-well box of cookies if a client is under the weather or recovering from a procedure. If your firm has some cool new swag—maybe a high-quality phone charger—don't wait for a special occasion. Just send it to your clients to let them know you value them all year!

When the holidays do roll around, I love sending gift packs of wine from Selby winery in California (no relation!) to my clients. My clients really appreciate the gesture and get a kick out of seeing my name on the label!

Don't Procrastinate

Don't procrastinate or agonize over figuring out the perfect way to start building relationships in your industry. While you're taking days to formulate the 100 percent perfect email to invite a prospective to meet for dinner at that next big industry conference, your competition has already done that, and you are too late.

Time and time again, I've seen partners procrastinate with their business-development activities due to insecurity that is often masked as perfection. Find your confidence to make the ask in the knowledge that you're good at what you do, and you have a heart to provide the best service to your clients.

Playing the Inside Game Well

Being a partner with responsibility for client relationships and business development doesn't mean that you can act like a free agent within your law firm. To be successful, you must continue to do the things that helped you achieve partnership in the first place. This means having an ownership mentality, and being a good "firm citizen" and someone your partners will want to work with. Being a successful partner also means serving as a role model to the firm's associates, managing a growing caseload well, and helping the firm to grow.

Don't Be a Jerk

It's unfortunate that it has to be said that being a partner is not a license to be entitled, throw temper tantrums, or be rude to staff, associates, or other partners. Again, think about the words you want people to use to describe you. I doubt you'd want to see "hothead" or "bully" on the list. Nor would you want to be described as emotional or on a power trip. There's no doubt that being a law firm partner is stressful, but your emotions do not entitle you to act like a child. You are not your feelings.

Associates today are much more likely to complain to firm management about abusive partners. This often opens a formal investigation involving firm leadership and HR. The allegedly offending partner is called into the managing partner's office, and an inquiry begins. The partner is often precluded from having any contact with that associate, at least during the pendency of the investigation. At a minimum, this can be highly embarrassing to the partner, but it can also cost him his job.

Don't let that be you. Today's legal and workplace environments rarely tolerate bullies, or conduct that is rude and aggressive. Don't be the partner whom associates and support staff hate or refuse to work with. I'm not saying that you should be a doormat and accept poor work or that you should be an emotionless robot, but you do need to find healthy and professional ways to deliver feedback and deal with your emotions. Go for a walk, drop and do a set of burpees, get a coach, or go to therapy.

Remember that even one emotional outburst can do real damage to your reputation and career. Discipline your emotions and keep yourself in check before your partners or firm management has to do that for you.

Learn How to Delegate

Delegation of work to junior associates is absolutely crucial to your ability to grow and scale your practice. This can be especially challenging, especially if you tend to be a perfectionist or have trust issues. But delegating work to others is really the only way to grow and scale your practice and develop firm associates.

Do your best not to micromanage, and accept that mistakes are inevitable. Improve your ability to provide clear and helpful instructions when reviewing and editing the work of junior attorneys, and provide constructive feedback.

I had a great relationship for years with an industry colleague before we started to work together at the same law firm. After we joined forces, I soon realized that she was a chronic complainer and needed almost constant reassurance.

It wasn't long before I started to distance myself from her, not having the time or energy to spend hours each week listening to her complain. Especially because she never would take the bull by the horns or actually do anything to improve her situation. I was on a mission to build my own practice, and this woman was draining the life and energy out of me.

It can be very difficult to overcome a reputation for being an "energy suck." So, don't get that reputation in the first place! Don't complain to your partners or escalate every problem, perceived slight, or conflict to firm management. This reeks of insecurity and a sad need for attention. And it exhausts the people around you. Instead, pick your battles wisely and don't be the high-maintenance or "difficult" partner.

If you're struggling to deal with the challenges of being a partner, it's up to you to look for ways to up your game. Consider taking courses or reading books on sales, management, leadership, and having difficult conversations.

Personally, I took Darren Hardy's "Hero's Journey" leadership course a few years ago, and it comprehensively covered virtually every aspect of leadership and business development. I highly recommend it.

Continue to Be a Good "Firm Citizen"

Your obligation to follow the rules does not end when you become a partner. In fact, you take on additional responsibilities. For example, as a partner, you will be privy to confidential information about the firm's finances and strategic plans, budgeting, compensation, and personnel issues involving other partners, associates, and employees. This information must be kept confidential.

You also have an obligation to serve the firm well in ways that will not show up as billable time. Volunteer for firm committees that are well suited to your skill set and personality. For instance, you might be an excellent person to lead the mentoring committee. Or, if you have a good head for numbers and are knowledgeable about the legal marketplace, you might be a good fit for the compensation committee.

Adopt a role model mentality. Brendan Burchard, the famous high-performance coach, defines a "role model mentality" as a decision and intention that you're going to be a force for positivity and good influence. Be the type of partner that associates, and even other partners, aspire to be.

Look for opportunities to provide spontaneous mentoring. Taking a moment to acknowledge something great or to point out an area for improvement can have a profound impact on an associate. Personally, I'm still driven by the spontaneous mentoring that certain partners chose to share with me when I first started practicing. Spontaneous mentoring can be a zero-cost, high-impact way for you to use your position as a partner to develop today's associates into better professionals and tomorrow's partners.

Acquaint yourself with ethical obligations, including fiduciary duties, that are applicable to law firm partners. These rules can be particularly important if you're thinking of making a lateral move to another firm. These are a matter of state law, and so I would encourage you to do your research on what your precise obligations are.

Just like associates, partners must submit their time entries in a timely manner. But they must also submit required budgets, review invoices, complete associate and staff reviews, and other things in a timely manner. Partners also may have to assist with collections on overdue client invoices. Don't be the partner who is always late in getting their time in, finalizing their bills, and submitting required budgets.

Also, remember that business development is not a zero-sum game. Don't be the partner who doesn't share credit with other partners who help develop the new business or whose reputation, relationships, or expertise you leverage to get the new business.

Hone Your Expertise

Develop a reputation as the go-to lawyer in your area of expertise. This is key to achieving domain dominance in the market.

During a recent holiday catch-up call, I was chatting with a legal reporter in my industry about the latest cutting-edge developments and trends. She mentioned that she recently teed up one of those issues at a meeting with several industry leaders and asked if they had any insight to offer. They responded, "Call Judy about that. She knows everything!"

Well, I clearly don't know everything, and I appreciate that this was said in jest. But it really made my day. I have to admit that I take great pride in being knowledgeable in my area of expertise and being known for it.

Become a master of your work. Know the relevant case laws and regulations in your area. Keep track of developments as they happen. Be the first one to report on these new developments to your clients and potential clients.

Even though you may read *Law360* every morning, so does everyone else. Here are other ways you can develop cutting-edge expertise in your area:

- **Identify the key thought leaders in your field and follow them online.** It's usually easy to identify the major thought leaders in the various practice areas. They're typically the ones quoted in the press and speaking at major industry conferences. I recommend following them, or ideally, connecting with them on LinkedIn, and subscribing to their newsletters. Take advantage of the wisdom they share, which often is completely free to access.

- **Take courses and keep learning to stay current.** Depending on your practice area, you may want to take courses to ramp up your knowledge and add some distinguishing credentials to your bio. For me, I took several courses through the professional education program at the Massachusetts Institute of Technology (MIT) in areas related to my focus on cyber insurance. To say those were challenging courses would be a massive understatement. I paid for them myself, and I didn't even tell anyone when I was taking the first course in case I didn't pass. But the knowledge I gained from those courses was outstanding, and the certificates I received after successfully completing them were a terrific attention-getter and differentiator in my bio.

- **Take advantage of free content that's available online.** Read law firm blogs, including those from firms on the opposite side of the types of cases that you and your firm handle. Attend free webinars put on by experts in the space. Check out videos on YouTube and listen to podcasts. Read books. Read cases and treatises.

- **Set up Google Alerts for relevant stories and reports in your field.** Don't worry about being inundated with too much information. Simply refine your search terms. You'll also find that you'll soon become an expert at quickly weeding through the irrelevant content and zeroing in on what matters. If your firm offers knowledge-management services, lean into those resources.

- **Build your reputation by sharing what you know.** Write articles, and speak at seminars and conferences. Give presentations to current and potential clients concerning emerging legal trends in your space.

Stay in Your Lane

As personal branding expert Rory Vaden always says, diluted focus will give you diluted results. Focus maniacally on your domain, and work to make your name synonymous with that practice area. Don't try to be all things to all people.

Years ago, I had a personal goal to make my name synonymous with "cyber insurance." To do that, I went on a mission to learn as much as I could about the industry and issues that impact it, like cybersecurity, tech advances, privacy laws, alternative sources of insurance capacity, and litigation developments. Following this strategy, as well as conducting consistent content, marketing, and networking, I was honored as a Cyber Insurance Trailblazer in 2020, the Cyber Risk Attorney of the Year in 2023, and a leading LinkedIn Legal Influencer in 2024.

There's nothing wrong with being a generalist, but in my personal opinion, particularly in a Big Law setting, it's probably better to develop deep expertise in a specific area. Sophisticated clients tend to look for and value specialized knowledge.

Promote Your Partners, Not Just Yourself

One of the best things about being a law firm partner, instead of a solo practitioner, is that you're part of a team of lawyers, and each one brings a unique skill set and expertise to the table.

Being part of a team with diverse skill sets can enable you to better serve your clients if they have needs beyond your particular niche. It also enables you to make more money by being the partner who originates work for other firm lawyers.

Smart firms prioritize cross-marketing among the firm's partners. But how do you actually do it?

Step one is to study all the practice areas your firm specializes in, and to identify the key partners in each specialty. You can't cross-market or offer to make key introductions if you don't have this basic knowledge about your firm.

Do this proactively, not just after you're asked if your firm can assist with a particular matter or issue. The truth is that you never know when you may be asked for a referral that one of your partners is perfect for. Think how much better it would be if you could immediately respond to a referral question with a definitive answer like "Yes, my partner Abby specializes in that exact area," instead of "I'll have to check and get back to you."

But you don't even need to wait to be asked to offer a referral. If you have clients who work in one of your partner's areas of expertise, consider introducing them to the client so they can get to know each other and build a relationship. Invite them both to lunch or dinner. Make an email introduction. Forward your partner's latest article on a big development in that area. Even if your client uses another firm for that work, remember that conflict issues may arise, the other firm may fall out of favor, or their key partner may retire. You want your partner to be known and top of mind in such situations.

Action Steps

- Remember, no matter how junior or senior you are, you're in the service business. Let your clients know that you appreciate their business and do your best to make their jobs as easy as possible.

- Constantly look for ways to meet people in your industry and add value to them.

CHAPTER 5

Brand . . . and Rebrand

How can I make sure the right people know what I do?

Attorneys often believe that doing a good job is all that it takes to succeed in their careers. After all, good work speaks for itself, right?

Not exactly.

While excellent performance is crucial, in today's economy, it likely won't be enough to get you where you need to go. Clients need to know you exist. They need to know what you do. And they need to know why they should even consider working with you when there are so many other options in a crowded and competitive marketplace. Standing out from the pack can be challenging.

Whether it's a firm or an individual professional, the process of marketing for yourself as a lawyer has changed dramatically over the past few years. Gone are the days of simply updating a résumé to indicate your area of interest.

Merely adding a new practice or specialty to your firm's list of provided services is not likely to lure new clients. Employers and clients today go well past résumés and marketing slicks when vetting professionals.

They will google you, look you up on LinkedIn, and search other social media platforms for information about you. In fact, it's almost an absolute certainty that the first impression people have of you will be from an online search.

Without a doubt, your "personal brand" is likely to be a dispositive factor for people deciding whether or not to hire or do business with you. But what exactly is a personal brand, and how can you tailor yours to help you get exactly where you want to go?

What is a Personal Brand?

In the broadest sense, your "personal brand" is the way the world sees you. Career coach Tom Peters is credited with originating the term in a 1997 article in *Fast Company*, where he wrote, "Our most important job is to be head marketer for the brand called 'you.'"

But what is a personal brand? Jeff Bezos says it's what people say about you when you're not in the room. It defines the value that you bring to your target marketplace.

Your personal brand encompasses much more than what's on your CV or the homepage of your firm. It's comprised of a number of facets, including:

- Your online presence.
- The people and groups with whom you're connected.
- Your body of work, including content you've created.
- Your reputation among colleagues and peers.
- Your in-person presence, including the way you dress.
- Your voicemail greeting.
- Your email style.
- The way you design and keep up your office space.

A Look Inside the Firm

"Oh, you're the associate with the lamp!"

Right after I started at my first law firm, I went shopping for a desk lamp. My office could be a bit dark, and I thought a desk lamp would be a nice touch. After all, I was spending a lot of time there. I was intending to get a typical desk lamp. I came across a beautiful ceramic lamp (on sale) that just happened to match the office decor. I didn't have anything in mind when I got it, other than that I liked the lamp. And I didn't even realize until someone pointed out to me months later that the design on the lamp was actually golf symbols, which was great because I love golf!

I brought the lamp into my office and didn't really think much of it other than it looked good, and I liked the extra light. But everybody else noticed, including a senior partner, who passed by my office one day and poked her head in, saying, "Oh, you're the associate with the lamp! I love it!"

We ended up having a nice conversation about her practice and what I was doing. And it was great to have the opportunity to interact with a senior partner, who would have buzzed right past my office without saying a word, but for that lamp!

That little accessory made my office look different from all the others in a very good way. It sent a message, albeit unplanned, that this is someone who cares about her office and the environment that she's working in.

On the other hand, a messy office with papers and files all over the place (or worse, dirty cups and leftover lunches) can send a signal that you're sloppy and disorganized, which doesn't exactly scream out "competent attorney."

Decorating your office with family pictures, sports mementos, and the like, are great ways to show your personality and interests, and they can also be great conversation starters. My advice would be to do this in moderation. A cluttered office can give off the vibe of a disorganized mind. Again, this does not send a signal of competence.

Keep Your Digital Brand Up-to-Date

Even if you've never focused on it, you already have a personal brand. An incomplete or dated LinkedIn profile, or the absence of one altogether, may cause concern that you're out of touch and not plugged in to modern legal practice. A Google search that reveals only a link to your firm's website may be interpreted to mean that you are not well-known or seen as an expert in your practice area. An article on your firm's website last updated in 2015 may indicate that you're not up-to-date on the latest trends and developments.

In today's digital and hyper-connected society, this type of personal brand will do nothing to advance, and likely will impede, your chances of success. A personal brand demonstrating that you and your firm are respected, engaged, and well-connected experts in your chosen field will greatly improve the odds in your favor.

Develop an Effective Personal Brand

Building a brand for a practice group or an individual is a process, not a project. It requires patience, a well-designed and comprehensive plan, and a bit of trial and error.

But most importantly, it requires consistent action and commitment on your part. After all, as business consultant Ryan Lilly stated, "Personal brands are determined by a track record of actions, not a track record of plans."

Although the idea of creating a new personal brand may cause anxiety if you haven't previously focused on it, the great news is that you can take charge of your personal brand and design it however you see fit. It will take some work on your part, but developing a carefully designed personal brand will be well worth the effort you put into it.

An effective personal brand will:

- Boost your reputation and credibility.
- Improve your professional standing.
- Increase the chances that the right people will find you online.
- Grow your network and audience.
- Position you to engage with influencers and thought leaders in your new area.
- Create new opportunities.
- Allow you to stand out in the crowd.
- Provide you with career options.
- Create a hedge against business downturns and unexpected changes in employment status.
- Expedite your transition into your new target area.

The following are some key steps that both firms and individual lawyers can take to successfully brand themselves.

1. Commit to Credentialing

When a lawyer is looking to boost her reputation in a particular area, or looking to rebrand in a new direction, the move may be met with some skepticism. People may wonder if they are a "poser" just trying to ride an emerging wave. Do they really understand this new area, and will they be able to hit the ground running?

One of the best ways to demonstrate the necessary commitment, knowledge, and understanding is through credentialing.

There are a variety of options that you can take advantage of to demonstrate knowledge in a particular niche area of the law. For some specialties, an actual degree may be appropriate. For others, professional education options may be sufficient. There are numerous courses offered online, including those by prestigious universities, in a variety of fields.

From my area of focus, there are many options for advanced study in cyber and information security, privacy, and data science. Some courses are expensive but others may be free or at a low cost. Many provide a certificate of completion, which can be posted on your social media accounts and firm website.

Credentialing was an important early step in my personal plan to transition from general insurance coverage law to a demonstrated focus on cyber insurance. I took online courses at MIT on big data, cyber security, and the Internet of Things (IoT). I also took a week-long course at MIT on crisis management and disaster recovery. Surprisingly, out of over seventy students from twenty countries, I was the only lawyer in the class. I've also completed low-cost online courses on cloud computing and General Data Protection Regulation (GDPR) Data Protection Officer training. I've posted all these courses on my LinkedIn profile and included them in my bio.

My goal in taking these courses was not to become a tech wiz. I wanted to gain a deeper understanding of relevant technical issues, which, combined with my then twenty-five years of insurance coverage litigation experience, assisted me in communicating more effectively about technical issues with technical professionals.

Those credentials also helped me to stand out in a crowded marketplace. My MIT credentials, as well as my MIT connections, have proven to be more valuable than I ever could have anticipated, and have paid the price of tuition many times over.

Tips for Credentialing

- Explore resources like Coursera and EdX for potentially relevant courses.
- Take continuing legal education courses in new areas to develop your expertise.
- Check out courses and certifications offered by LinkedIn.

2. Develop an Effective Content Strategy

Executing an effective content strategy is probably the most important part of a successful professional branding process. Building a body of content is key to demonstrating in-depth knowledge, building a targeted network, and growing a new audience.

The concept of producing content in a new area can be intimidating. But the good news is that professionals, particularly lawyers, usually are extremely effective communicators, so this step should be less daunting for professionals than for others.

And the price is right: the cost to produce and share content is basically nothing. When you hear the word "content," you may automatically think of writing articles. Although creating original content for blogs and published articles likely will be a key component of your content strategy—as it was for me—it's only one of many content-creation techniques you can and should utilize. Others are:

- **Synthesizing:** Creating a useful summary of other people's articles, research, and studies. People are drowning in content, so something that can succinctly summarize a large or complex body of work can be of real value.

- **Interviewing:** Interviewing thought leaders can skyrocket your profile while also providing great content. Doing interviews is a great way to build relationships with prominent thought leaders and to be publicly associated with them.

- **Curating:** Sharing, commenting on, and liking other people's content is a fast and easy component of a good content strategy. It's also an important way to build your network.

Everyone loves when their contact is shared, reposted, and liked by their peers. Your content should be designed to attract your desired audience and address their questions and concerns, even if they're not yet aware of certain issues. For example, providing a heads-up about a likely new regulatory change or an impending legal decision provides value to your network and audience but also positions you as an expert of the subject matter.

But even the best content won't help to build your brand if nobody sees it. It's important to place your content where your desired audience can find it. This is where building a network comes into play, both in terms of getting good placements and sharing your content. Content-optimization tools may assist here as well. If you have access to PR professionals, they can help you identify and get placements in the right media outlets to reach your target audience.

Also consider subscribing to *Connectively* (formerly *HARO*: Help a Reporter Out), a free service used by reporters seeking quotes and interviews with subject-matter experts in a variety of fields for upcoming articles and news reports. There are frequent reporter requests in HARO for experts in the areas of cyber security, artificial intelligence, cryptocurrency, blockchain, cloud computing, and privacy regulations. Over the past few months, I have been quoted in several national publications via HARO.

My personal content strategy contains numerous components, including:

- Articles
- Webinars
- Daily LinkedIn posts
- Speaking events
- Podcasts
- Interviews (newspapers, magazines)
- Curating

I have found that writing articles (which takes the most time) leads to getting speaking engagements (which usually take less time), and the combination of those things leads to getting interviews (which take even less time). It's a super-efficient virtual cycle.

Tips to Maximize the Impact of Your Content:

- **Be consistent:** A good content strategy requires that you consistently and regularly provide valuable content. As I always say, consistency is a superpower!

- **Quality matters—a lot:** Your work should be accurate and well-written. You can do real damage to your new brand by generating sloppy or inaccurate content.

- **Be a reliable, trusted adviser:** This is essential to building a new network, audience, and successful brand.

- **Less is often more:** Unless you're writing for a formal journal or similar outlet, shorter content usually is more successful. Don't make the reader work to get through your content. There's too much competition for your audience's time and attention, and people will look elsewhere if it takes effort to read your content.

- **Don't overdo it:** Be thoughtful about the amount of content you're posting online. Don't clutter your followers' social media feeds by over-posting.

- **Stay in your lane:** The various sectors of professional services have a variety of components, but consider identifying a specific niche, developing a deep expertise in that niche, and limiting your content to that discreet area.

- **Keep it professional:** Weighing in on political and other controversial issues may be risky. When you're looking to develop a professional brand, it's probably best to stay on message and avoid the risk of diluting your message or alienating members of your desired network and audience by going off-brand, at least at the beginning of your career. I have seen other people take a different approach, so consider all your options and choose the one that's best for you. However, be super aware of how your strategy is playing out for you. If it's not well received, change it.

- **Keep your end goal in mind:** If you're posting to build your brand as a competent, high-level attorney, you may want to resist the urge to chase likes by posting on issues that are unrelated to the professional brand you're trying to build.

3. Build Your Network

Building a network in your target area is a critical component of a successful branding process. For our purposes, network means the people you know, or with whom you're connected online.

For example, your network includes your colleagues and peers, your connections and followers on social media such as LinkedIn, Instagram, and Facebook, as well as people who subscribe to your newsletter. In other words, your network consists of people with whom you have some sort of direct connection.

The benefits of building a network in your target area are immense. You can learn from and share ideas with your network connections. They can provide you with guidance, mentorship, and sponsorship. They can endorse you, share your content, introduce you to others in the field, bring opportunities to you, partner with you on content creation, and more.

Each member of your network can become an invaluable ambassador of your brand. Today's network connection may be tomorrow's business partner, referral source, or client.

In today's marketplace, social media is the optimal tool for network building. I have "met" people through social media with whom I have partnered on articles and webinars, but we still have not met in person. We socialize each other's content, write reviews of each other's books, and refer business to each other. These relationships are the result of developing my personal brand and using social media consistently.

LinkedIn is a particularly valuable tool for today's lawyers. To set the right tone, make sure your profile is up-to-date and relevant. A current, professional photo is a must. Maximize the "headline" section of your profile by highlighting your areas of expertise as opposed to simply stating that you're an associate or partner at your firm.

Frequently update your bio to reflect your credentials, projects, publications, and speaking engagements, and work hard to build up your connections. A deficient or dated LinkedIn profile, or one with a paltry number of connections, is likely to send a negative signal to an audience.

For attorneys, it also may be helpful to have your own website. You will want to post your own content on your website, but you also can ask others for permission to post their content on your site. Not only are people typically flattered by this type of request, which can lead to the development of good personal relationships, but it also affords you the opportunity to be publicly branded and associated with prominent thought leaders.

A word of caution: Lawyers should consult with their firms about starting an individual website, and they should be careful to avoid legal, business, and other types of conflicts with firm clients.

Although online networking is crucial, the importance of in-person network development should not be forgotten. There is no shortage of business-related conferences, so make sure to do some due diligence and focus on the most appropriate conferences to reach your target network.

Attending and speaking at the right events can jump-start your network-building process, especially if you combine those activities with your online networking efforts.

Do your homework before you attend in-person events by researching who is speaking and attending. Make a list of people you'd like to meet and do your best to meet them. Create social media posts in advance, during, and after the event, in which you can highlight your role at the conference and give a "shout-out" or "thank-you" to speakers and other attendees.

After the event, follow up online with the people you met and invite them to connect on LinkedIn. Even if you were unable to personally meet everyone on your target list, send them a LinkedIn invitation, noting that you tried to connect at the event, you enjoyed their remarks (if they were a speaker), and that you'd like to connect with them online.

When building a network, it's important not to focus exclusively on potential clients. Other service providers are often well-positioned to refer work and provide speaking and writing opportunities to other professionals, even competitors, whom they know and trust.

Tips to build and maintain your network:

- **Look for ways to *give*, not *get*.** Ask what you can do to help others achieve their goals.

- **Avoid shameless self-promotion.** Some experts recommend that no more than 10 percent of your social media posts should be some form of self-promotion.

- **Turn contacts into real relationships.** Connect and converse online, and look for ways to support their brand.

- **Utilize a customer relationship management system (CRM).** Develop a routine for staying in touch. Invite people to events and webinars, and send holiday cards.

- **Constantly update and maintain your online profile.** Your new contacts are likely to look at your social media profiles, particularly LinkedIn, and will google you before or after your first meeting. This is your opportunity to brand yourself as you want to be seen.

- **Stay consistent across social media platforms.** Utilize the same professional picture, and maintain a consistent style and theme.

- **Don't neglect in-person meetings.** Face-to-face contact can help to build lasting impressions and relationships.

4. Build Your Audience

Don't confuse your network with your audience. While your network is composed of somewhat personal connections, your audience is a much broader group of people in your target area. For example, a politician's network may be made up of other politicians, supporters, and donors, while her audience is all registered voters. You will want to find ways to reach the target audience of people who might hire you, but your network is likely to contain other service providers, reporters, editors, conference promoters, and industry association employees.

Tips to build your target audience:

- **Figure out how to get in front of your desired clients.** Look to place your content in the publications they read. It's important to be authentic, but to a degree, you should mimic the style of successful content providers in those publications. For instance, if your goal is to publish in an academic journal, your style will be very different from someone writing a short blog post.

- **Always follow the submission and editorial guidelines the publication provides.** Otherwise, you risk your submission being returned for editing or even rejected.

- **Identify the conferences that your targets attend.** Do some research to figure out the conferences that your targets attend.

Conference attendees and speakers often post on LinkedIn about their plans to be at certain events, so use that as a resource.

- **Identify what mediums of content your audience prefers (written, video, podcasts, or images).** This likely will involve some trial and error, but in my experience, videos and images are typically well-received.

- **Identify the style of content that resonates best with your audience.** This also is a trial and error process, but generally, short content is likely to do better with busy professionals.

- **Identify and connect with your audience's thought leaders.** Online searches, including on LinkedIn, should make this process fairly easy.

- **Identify key issues or pain points for which they need a solution and provide it.** This may be by publishing a compendium of new regulations, informing them about relevant legal decisions, regulatory or legislative developments, or partnering with technical resources to offer a comprehensive solution to existing problems.

- **Identify relevant professional organizations and get involved in a substantive way.** This will depend on your area of expertise, but the key is to actually get involved to build your knowledge, brand, and relationships. Volunteer for committees, offer to provide written content, or co-chair an event. There are many options, but finding the right organization for you and growing with it can be a career game changer.

5. Be Prepared to Explain Your New Brand

If you decide to change the focus of your career, you'll need to do some advanced planning to rebrand yourself effectively. As an experienced attorney looking to transition into a new area, you'll need to do more than simply become well-versed in a new area of the law. You may also have to explain to potential new clients, or to a new employer, why you're looking to move into a new practice area.

This is especially true if you're coming from a markedly different area. Expect to be asked about this. In addition to being able to recite your qualifications in this new field, be ready to provide a brief but compelling reason for your career transition.

Perhaps there are ways that your prior legal experience complements your new specialty, or provides you with connections to target clients or business sectors. Or maybe you, or someone close to you, had an experience with a relevant issue that gave you the impetus to transition.

Think about your "why" in advance, and be prepared to allay any concerns about your qualifications, dedication, and value proposition.

The good news is that your online brand is almost entirely within your control. Implement these five steps to guide your efforts to develop a thoughtful brand strategy that complements your personality type and personal strengths.

Some Thoughts about LinkedIn

For many lawyers, LinkedIn is the premiere social media platform for brand building and networking. But that doesn't mean there aren't risks to using LinkedIn. Consider these points before engaging:

- **Use caution when reaching out to someone.** In most cases, it's probably a mistake to directly message someone whom you don't know, or have not been in contact with for a while, and ask them to make connections or introductions for you, or even worse, ask them to hire you.

- **Build a relationship by adding value before asking for favors from people on LinkedIn.** I recently accepted a connection request from a former college professor who now works as an expert witness. I thought it would be interesting to see what kind of content he shared online. Instead, he immediately emailed me and asked me to introduce him to partners in my law firm. I did not respond. He emailed me twice more, getting a bit more insistent each time, basically demanding that I introduce him to partners in my law firm. I absolutely do not recommend this approach. His behavior and bad judgment made it much more likely that I would advise my partners to steer away from him.

- **Do your best to vet people before you connect with them on LinkedIn.** Unfortunately, there are scammers and fake profiles on LinkedIn. If a random person you don't know asks to connect with you, run a Google search for them and their company. A connection request from someone with no online history other than a LinkedIn account with very few connections is a major red flag. Don't feel compelled to connect with just anyone because you want to have more connections.

- **You may have to block certain connections on LinkedIn.** I recently blocked someone who routinely posted snarky comments on LinkedIn posts, including mine, concerning a particular legal issue. I tolerated it for a while, and then I finally had to block him. His comments became a distraction and added no value. I later learned that I was hardly the first person to do that!

Action Steps

- Do something every day to promote your brand in the marketplace.

- Focus on the process, not the results, and practice proactive patience. Consistency is the key, even when the results are slow to materialize.

- Demonstrate your expertise by providing valuable information and assistance to people in your network and audience. Look to give, not get.

CHAPTER 6

Get Out of Your Own Way

How do I bring my best self to work every day?

I'm from a hardworking family. Nothing was handed to us. Money was tight. No one was coming in to clean the house, iron the clothes, wash the windows, mow the lawn, or shovel the snow in the winter. We did it all ourselves.

We walked over an hour each day to and from the subway because we didn't have enough money for both the bus and the train fare. We "brown-bagged" it instead of buying lunch at the school cafeteria. We were raised to be competent, and we did what had to be done. And most importantly, throughout all this, we became very comfortable with being uncomfortable.

The most successful attorneys I have ever met are also very comfortable at being uncomfortable. They travel even when they don't want to. They get up early and stay up late. They work weekends when they have to. They attend networking events. They write the articles, ask for the business, and maintain a level of energy that enables them to do this over the course of many years.

In other words, they do the things that other attorneys simply are not willing to do.

But why is that? Why are some attorneys willing to go to the networking event on a cold and rainy night, make follow-up calls afterward, send

LinkedIn invitation requests, and ask for the work, while so many others do not? Why are some attorneys so consistent with their business-development activities while most are not?

During business planning and development meetings, I would hear the same thing over and over again from certain colleagues: "I really should start posting, networking, following up, to build my business," followed by, "I'll do it tomorrow." And tomorrow never comes.

To reach your potential and be the most successful attorney you can be, you're going to have to do things that you don't want to do, and you're going to have to do them consistently. Whether you like it or not. Whether you feel like it or not. Whether you're in the mood or not.

But how do you do that? How do you make yourself consistently post on LinkedIn, make that call to ask for business or for a meeting, invite that potential client out to lunch, or walk into a networking event where you don't know a single person, when you just don't feel like doing it?

Here's the secret.

You need to connect to your driving force, your *burn*.

Your Burn

Tapping into your burn can give you the push you need to do things you otherwise simply would not do. But what is your burn? Discovering the answer to this question may require a lot of introspection.

Ben Newman, one of *USA Today*'s Top 5 Performance Coaches, says the burn is more than your "why" and your purpose. But it ignites your "why" and purpose and drives you to consistently perform at your highest level.

For some people, their burn might be to prove wrong that person who said they wouldn't amount to anything. Or maybe you want to be the one who finally pulls your family out of poverty. Perhaps you need to pay your kids' medical bills, or you want to retire your parents after they worked hard their whole lives for you.

Your burn may even be something totally materialistic, like really wanting to buy a new house or a new car. Or it could be a deep belief in your client's cause or legal case.

For me, it's to honor the gifts and talents I've been blessed with, and to honor the sacrifices that others have made for me. To me, this is a sacred obligation, encapsulated in Luke 12:48 *"For everyone who has been given much, much will be demanded; and from the one who has been entrusted with much, much more will be asked."*

Whatever it is for you, it should transcend your feelings and emotions. It should trigger something deep inside you so that when you think about it, you can do hard things. You can force yourself to do them even though you don't like it.

You already know, intellectually, that you should go to that networking event and start engaging with potential clients and industry players that you don't really know.

But that intellectual "knowing" may not be enough to make you actually do it! That's when you have to connect with your burn, which will give you the drive and the "why" you need to do it.

To really capture and leverage the power of your burn, you need to keep it in front of you. Make thinking about it, connecting with it, part of your daily routine.

Try writing it down every morning when you wake up and right before you go to bed for the next thirty days. Write it on Post-it notes and put them throughout your house and on your computer. Make it a screensaver on your phone. The more you focus on it, the more it will get into your subconscious, so when you even think about not doing something that you should, your burn will trigger you to do it.

Managing the Stress

As a lawyer, at every stage of your career, there will be no shortage of high stress and difficult issues to deal with. The attorneys who handle those situations well will do better in every aspect of their careers.

Here are the steps I've taken throughout my legal career to deal with stressful situations, maintain my focus, and consistently show up and perform.

- **Stay in Shape**

Prioritize your health and exercise. Eat well and put your workouts on your schedule. Many of the most successful people in the world are known for their morning routines, including 5:00 a.m. workouts. Why do they do it so early? Because it's a priority for them, and it's time they can control.

They're less likely to run into scheduling conflicts at 5:00 a.m. and put it off. The workout actually gets done.

The benefits of these early-morning workouts are more than improved physical health. First off, these early-morning warriors start their day with a win and get into the right mindset to start their day strong.

Also, people who are in great shape tend to be more confident, and project an air of vitality and energy that is attractive to other people. Plus, the mental health benefits of exercise are well documented.

If you are having trouble pushing yourself to get your workouts in, remember your burn and use it as fuel to discipline yourself. The great thing about using your burn to consistently show up is that you'll soon develop an automatic habit that you don't have to think about, let alone push yourself to do.

Exercise will become part of your identity as a person. And it will help you succeed as an attorney, especially as you get older.

I'm not exactly proud of the fact that I've worked through, quite literally, recoveries from two knee replacements, a reverse shoulder replacement, and an ankle reconstruction all over the second half of my career. Aside from the surgery days, I did not take time off and continued to work while I was home recovering. I'm 100 percent confident that I would not have been able to do that if I was not comfortable being uncomfortable and had not prioritized health and fitness my entire life.

For me, my ideal routine is early-morning workouts with cardio and weight training, in addition to lots of dog walks and healthy-lifestyle decisions throughout the day, like taking the stairs instead of the elevator, taking long walks through the airport when waiting for a flight, and parking far away from the entrance to a building or store.

By the way, I routinely get teased quite a bit about my early wake-up time, but I really don't care! I believe it has played a huge part in my success over the past three decades.

- **Look for the Opportunity**

Simply dealing with stress is one thing, but how about finding ways to make stressful events actually work in your favor? By looking for the opportunity in every situation, you can do exactly that!

One time I was involved in a difficult matter, and eventually, the tension level between my client and the other party in the case started to go off the charts. They'd absolutely had it with each other.

One afternoon, as I rushed through an airport to board a flight, I dreaded the call I had to make to my opposing counsel in a few hours when I landed. But instead of focusing on how annoying the call was likely to be, I took a deep breath and asked myself, *What is the opportunity in this situation?* It took only a minute before I got my answer. I would be the person who actually reduces the tension level and gets the case back on track toward settlement.

Approaching the phone call with that mindset was a complete game changer. It was well received by my opposing counsel, and together, we worked to bring our clients back to the settlement table.

When you're facing any type of difficulty or problem, ask yourself *What is the opportunity in this situation?* Or *What is one thing I can do to improve this situation?*

Simply asking yourself questions like this will put you in a more positive and resourceful mindset, which instantly forces your brain to start looking for answers that can empower you to take positive action. I have found that taking action in a positive direction often is the best way to eliminate stress.

- **Avoid Unhealthy Outlets for Stress**

At all costs, avoid turning to negative or unhealthy habits to deal with stress. Complaining to your colleagues may feel good at first, but it does nothing to move the ball forward, and you start to get a reputation of being a complainer and a time suck—an "energy vampire," as Jon Gordon says.

Having a drink in an attempt to avoid the issue, or to decompress or relax can be even worse. Statistics show that substance abuse among attorneys is a very real issue and can lead to problems with your health, in your relationships, and in your career.

- **Feed Your Mind the Right Things**

In addition to taking care of your body, it's just as important to take care of your mind. What are you feeding your mind on a daily basis? What, and who, are you listening to all day? And what are you saying to yourself all day long?

Fill your mind with positive messages that empower you and awaken your unique talents and resourcefulness. Personally, I avoid the news as much as possible, and years ago, went cold turkey off my daily routine of watching political news every morning.

Instead, I devour personal development and spiritual content in books, podcasts, and YouTube videos. I read a personally curated list of inspiring quotes that inspire and guide me every morning, as well as two devotionals. I consciously practice gratitude and engage in positive and empowering self-talk throughout the day.

These activities are not random or something I do when I feel like it or if I happen to remember. They are scheduled, high-priority activities that I do first thing every day. There are no days off, including when I'm traveling or if

I have an early meeting. I'm never too busy for this. This practice gets me in the best mindset to head into each day.

As you go through your work day, make a point to look for positive things. Don't be on the lookout for things to be offended by, which is a terrible way to live. And do your best to focus only on things you can control and then actually take action to control them.

Throughout the day, keep your goals top of mind. I suggest writing them down and reading them multiple times every day. And take steps every day in the direction of your goals. By regularly focusing on your goals, the reasons you do what you do, you're less likely to get derailed by the distractions, pressures, and annoyances that inevitably crop up each day.

One of the best ideas I've ever come up with to protect my mindset and keep me moving in the right direction was deciding not to say certain things. I actually have a list of things I simply do not say. I started the list many years ago before I even thought about going to law school, and it has served me well for decades. I have come to believe that saying negative things makes them become a self-fulfilling prophecy, and I can't do what I need to do if I'm poisoning my mind with negative self-talk.

The first thing on my never-say-it list is "I'm tired." But the most impactful thing on my list has been, "I don't feel like it." Think about it. When do people say that? It's almost always when they're talking about doing something they know they should do but would prefer not to. If you think back over the past few years, imagine what your life would be like now if you had actually done all the things—made all the calls, went to the gym, attended all the events, wrote the articles, posted on LinkedIn—that you didn't do, just because you didn't "feel like it."

A Look Inside the Firm

"I'm So Tired."

I was working with a guy who was very sweet but constantly complained about how tired he was. And I do mean constantly. Every morning, he would come to work and say, "I'm so tired, I'm so tired." Just hearing this was exhausting to everyone he worked with!

One day, after listening again to his now-familiar refrain, I vowed to never say the words "I'm tired" ever again. No matter how I feel. No matter how much sleep I didn't get.

- **Give Back**

One of the best ways you can deal with stress is to look for ways to give back. Focusing on others instead of yourself, and using your gifts and talents to make someone else's life better, can be a game changer.

Consider pro bono work or coaching a team. Mentor underprivileged kids. Raise money for causes you believe in. Walk dogs at the local animal shelter.

Looking to give will get you out of your head and help you to better appreciate your own life and view your problems through a better perspective.

- **Boost Your Self-Confidence**

Many lawyers that I've worked with over the years simply lack the self-confidence to take the necessary action to build their business, which adds to their stress and anxiety levels. Ed Mylett, the successful entrepreneur and success coach, says something that really resonates with me about this. He says, "When you keep promises to the most important person on earth, which is you… [you will] build your self-confidence… [and] set yourself up for one hell of an awesome life."

By actually doing the things you say you will, like going to the gym, completing the first draft of that research memo or attending the networking event, you strengthen the relationship you have with yourself, and you build your own credibility. Doing this helps you develop your self-confidence.

You simply can't divorce self-confidence from self-discipline. It's hard to feel good about yourself if you are routinely not doing things you know you should do. Unlike your self-worth --your innate value as a human being -- your self-confidence must be earned. Doing what you know you should do, regardless of your feelings, silences self-doubt and builds self-confidence. It's a virtuous cycle.

But when people don't keep the promises they make to themselves, the negative self-talk often begins: *I'm such a loser. Why can't I do what I'm supposed to do? Why am I so lazy?*

Keeping your commitments changes everything. *I actually did what I said I would do. I'm so glad I forced myself to go to that event.*

Try this for two weeks. Pick one thing you know you should do, but for whatever reason, you just haven't been doing it. Commit to keeping your word to yourself for the next fourteen days and see the difference it makes in your self-confidence and your stress levels.

- **Make a Game Plan for Downtime**

A very stressful time for lawyers can be when they don't have a lot of billable work to do. You may have just settled a big case that consumed all your time for months, or you happen to settle a few cases at the same time, or you're in the process of building a new practice at the firm, which can take a long time.

Regardless of the reasons, there are expectations and requirements for a minimum number of billable hours, typically even for partners. And not having billable time to enter every day on your timesheet can really weigh on your mind. So, what can you do to make the situation better?

Think about creating a high-value action plan in advance of any downtime you can use to generate new business. Are there clients, or potential clients, who you can take out to lunch? Can you write an article on a cutting-edge issue in your practice area? Can you set up presentations for clients and prospective clients concerning emerging issues in your area?

Presentations like this are a great way to provide added value to your clients, demonstrate your expertise, and remain top of mind with current and potential clients, even if the time is not billable.

Taking actions like these can reduce the anxiety of having downtime. Make a plan to use the time to build your brand, deepen relationships, and develop new business.

Just having a plan you can implement reduces stress. Just getting started reduces stress. Taking action reduces stress. Being prepared to do these things reduces stress.

- **Develop an End-of-Day Stress Reduction Routine**

Before you walk away from your desk at the end of the day, take a sticky note and list the three most important things you need to do in the morning. Just putting this down on paper can prevent your brain from ruminating on those things as you try to turn off work for the day.

As you're getting ready to go to bed each night, ask yourself, "What are three things I did well today?" This will help you to focus on the positives and what you're proud of at the end of the day. Think about these empowering wins instead of what went wrong. This will silence the inner critic, help you relax, and gain positive momentum as you head into the new day.

- **Preparing on Sunday Eliminates New Week Stressors**

Take some time on Sundays to plan out your priorities for the week, including your non-work priorities, which attorneys often fail to do. Remember, things you schedule are much more likely to actually get done. This includes your workouts, plans with family or friends, or reading that book you've been meaning to get to. I like to use the Ink & Vault 52-week dashboard planner for this.

Going into the week with a plan helps to keep you on track with your personal and professional goals and priorities. You're less likely to forget or procrastinate on tasks that are written into your plan. Knowing your game plan as you head into the new week is a great way to increase your productivity and shut down the Sunday Scaries.

- **Leverage "I Am" Statements to Ward off Stress**

One of the best ways to position yourself to handle stress well is to leverage the incredible power of "I am" statements. Positive "I am" statements can shape your self-perception and beliefs, influence your mindset, and build on your confidence so that you're well-equipped to endure the rigors of a Big Law practice. Some of my favorite "I am" statements are:

- I am loved, protected, guided, and promoted.
- I am well able to achieve my goals.
- I am uncommon, not average.
- I am a "doer," not a "wisher."

Think of some "I am" statements that resonate with you, things that empower you, energize you, and make you feel like your best self. Get in the habit of saying them to yourself throughout the day, every day. As Pastor Steven Furtick says, "If you argue for your limitations, you get to keep them." I propose that you use "I am" statements to argue for your opportunities and keep those instead. Internalizing positive "I am" statements can be a powerful tool to help you cope with the inevitable pressures of a legal practice.

- **Laugh!**

The practice of law is serious business, but that doesn't mean it can't be fun. Make a conscious effort to bring some fun into your daily work. Try to socialize with your colleagues and keep things light. Don't take yourself too seriously, and affirmatively decide that you will look for ways to bring joy to your work.

Action Steps

- The gateways to long-term success are a positive mindset, a heart to serve others, and a fit and healthy body. Develop and prioritize the routines that work best for you to achieve these outcomes.

- Consistently feed your mind with positive, encouraging messages.

- Look for the opportunity in every challenging situation. It's always there!

Conclusion

This book stands as a testament to the transformative power—even in the legal profession—of a blue-collar work ethic. My message is clear: Success throughout your career requires more than pedigree—it demands resilience, determination, and a relentless pursuit of excellence—always remembering that your work is in service to others.

As you embark on your own journey, my prayer is that the lessons and wisdom in this book will serve as a road map that guides you and enables you to develop the mindset you'll need to thrive through the adversity and challenges you'll inevitably encounter, always looking for the opportunity that's disguised as a problem.

Please remember, no matter where you come from or where you went to school, it's your work ethic and mindset that will ultimately determine your trajectory. With that, I invite you to embrace the lessons within these pages and forge ahead with confidence, knowing that your path to success is paved with hard work, determination, and your commitment to excellence.

Recap

Keep these 6 Questions in mind to guide you throughout your legal career.

6 Questions to Ignite Your Legal Career

1. How can I make this firm fall in love with me?
2. How can I make the partners' jobs easier?
3. How can I demonstrate that I'm ready for partnership?
4. How can I show appreciation for my clients and make their jobs easier?
5. How do I get the right people to know what I do?
6. How can I bring my best self to my job every day, year after year?

THANK YOU FOR READING MY BOOK!

Thank you for reading my book! Here are a few free bonus resources.

Scan the QR Code Here:

I appreciate your interest in my book and value your feedback as it helps me improve future versions of this book. I would appreciate it if you could leave your invaluable review on Amazon.com with your feedback. Thank you!